SEEING ANEW

Awakening to Life's Lessons

MARTINA LEHANE SHEEHAN

VERITAS

Published 2012 by
Veritas Publications
7–8 Lower Abbey Street
Dublin 1
publications@veritas.ie
www.veritas.ie

ISBN 978 1 84730 396 7

10 9 8 7 6 5 4 3 2 1

Cover design by Dara O'Connor, Veritas Publications
Printed in the Republic of Ireland by
Hudson Killeen Ltd, Dublin

DEDICATION

I dedicate this book to the memory of my mother, Anne, who had the gift of words and the gift of writing. *Mam, life didn't give you the opportunity to write your book and few people got to read your unique words of wisdom (which you called your 'scribbling'). But on the morning of my last birthday, I sensed your spirit nudging me to write something.* What was I to write, I wondered? I felt it was to be something about life's lessons, the universal search for happiness and meaning in all life's twists and turns. What I didn't realise then was that it would be my poor ankle that was to endure the twist and turns some months later, whereby an enforced period of inactivity cornered me into finally doing some scribbling. *And so, Mam, I hope your own unwritten book is in here too somewhere.*

May this book be guided by the 'inner light' that my mother discovered in the last years of her life. When I asked her about it, she said, 'I cannot describe this light, but if you ask, you will receive it also.' And so, this book is a search for that light which is available to all of us.

I am eternally grateful to those who patiently walk with me each day in this search, those who steer me towards the light, who help me to see anew. This book is dedicated to each of you.

Martina Lehane Sheehan
August 2012

ACKNOWLEDGEMENTS

A special thank you to all who have supported me on the journey, this book is a product of your presence in my life. To my friends, family, colleagues who have graced this book with the wisdom I have learnt from them. To those who read the first draft and challenged my self doubt by encouraging me to publish, especially to Anne Alcock, Benedict Hegarty OP, Claire O'Connell, Fr Daniel J. O'Leary, Sr Stanislaus Kennedy, who offered their professional opinion. To Veritas Publications, with whom I have enjoyed a most professional, yet gracious working relationship. And finally, to my husband Pat, for his unwavering support, and for his belief in *Seeing Anew*, long before it appeared in written form.

It is because I have been blessed, that I am choosing to donate my proceeds from sale of this book to Chernobyl Children International fund.

CONTENTS

Foreword

'Just a bit of writing' was how Martina Lehane Sheehan described the pages she was asking me to 'glance over'. It wasn't too long before I was on the phone to her. 'This is a *book*! It's ready to go! You have to publish it!' No doubt others went on to say the same, including my ninety-seven-year-old mother, who expressed great satisfaction in her read-through 'This is a book I can understand!'

'Understandable' it is, not only because of the vivid and humorous story-snapshots that my mother loved, but because each story conveys a flash of insight into aspects of our own lives that most prefer to gloss over. It is the truthfulness embedded in each chapter and section that gives this book its unique mix of lightness and gravitas; that allows a seamless blending of scripture, spirituality and psychological awareness and also useful teaching. This comes, of course, from Martina's own trainings, and growings, some of which it has been my privilege to witness at different life-stages over the past twenty-five years. In all that time, Martina was learning lessons that come from not running away, from not being able to run away, from staying and being with 'what is', all that makes up on-going life.

This means that she can dare to write from and about real pain and real suffering, with a raw directness. Then, sensitively illustrating the retrospective experience the title of the book implies, she attends to the wisdom gleaned. In a different tone and pace, the reader equally senses something of her grasp of the mystery and yet the presence of God, the experience of surrender, of letting go, and of contemplation.

Although the book has a unity and a flow, it is also possible, because of Martina's unique style, to take each chapter all by itself. Each chapter concludes with a reflection. These offer a practical application, such as meditative walking, or relaxing breath-work, or quiet remembering of one's own story. I find this so very well-handled, precisely because this is flowing from the author's daily work and personal experience.

Interspersed with Martina's own thoughtful reflections are a few short nuggets of wisdom from philosophers, poets and other spiritual authors. Above all though, the ultimate underpinning of this book is found in the living word of scripture making its home in the author and the reader and bringing forth fruit – fruit that will last.

I know that when I thanked her for the first sightings of what was to become this book, I said, 'I'm not sure I expected to, but in this, I've found I learned something.'

Anne Alcock
August 2012

Introduction

*And the day came when the risk it took to remain
tight in a bud was more painful than the risk it took
to blossom.*[1]

ANAÏS NIN

The day comes to all of us when we see the choice – to
embrace all that life is teaching, or to stay tightly
contracted against it. This awakening doesn't happen
on just one day, it happens every day, every moment –
whenever we have eyes to see the invitation offered to us, to
transcend the *tight bud* and allow our souls *to blossom*. We are
not asked to get it right, we are asked to be open, to keep the
heart soft, and in this open space we discover the healing and
stillness we long for. Maybe life is simply asking that we not
anesthetise ourselves against the bigger questions, but with
pilgrim hearts be always asking that which the poet Mary
Oliver asks: 'What is it you plan to do with your one, wild and
precious life?'[2]

The chapters of this book contain some of the lessons life
continually tries to teach us. Sometimes we 'listen and listen,
but never understand, look and look, but never perceive' (Mt

---

[1] As quoted in Dan Millman, *Living on Purpose: Straight Answers to Universal
Questions* (Novato, CA: New World Library, 2000), p. 4.
[2] Mary Oliver, 'The Summer Day', *New and Selected Poems*, Vol. 1 (Boston: Becon
Press, 1992), p. 94.

13:15-17), so the lessons repeat many times. Thankfully, Divine Providence is much more gentle with us than we are with ourselves. My wish is that these chapters act as a catalyst – a springboard for your own discovery of the wonderful treasures hidden in your unique, wild and precious life and in everyday events. So familiar are we with the landscape of our lives and stories that we often miss those treasures. Incidents and circumstances that seemed to have little relevance start to assume significance and become filled with meaning when we begin to see with the eyes of the soul.

The opening chapters speak to the child we once were, the child that lives on in our hearts. 'Our guru is the child within – small and simple and without pretence, who would have us reach out in a tender, healing touch, without our left hand knowing what our right hand is doing.'[3]

A lot of what shapes us come from our childhood memories, alongside those places and circumstances the ego would consider 'insignificant'. The wisdom these chapters may offer is not an infallible, absolute type of knowledge, but more an inner knowing, and a gentle prompt to help you on your life's journey. We are all learning, and we are always beginners when it comes to life's lessons and so it would be tragic to give up on the questions, to lose the magic and to lose the fire. I hope something from these chapters rekindles a little of that fire and magic for you.

Other chapters speak of some of my 'conversion' experiences, which have come about in tiny breakthroughs, chance encounters and everyday experiences. This is probably true for you also.

Some stories come from those whose lives I have had the privilege of being part of – colleagues, friends, clients and fellow travellers. Wherever I have shared something from someone else's life, I have sought their permission, and when appropriate masked their identity to protect confidentiality. The

---

[3] James Finley, *Merton's Palace of Nowhere* (Notre Dame, IN: Ave Maria Press, 1978), p. 81.

themes are universal: our search for wisdom, healing and happiness through all of life – through our joy, suffering and losses, as well as our longing for belonging and for a sense of purpose in our lives.

No longer content to learn about 'truth' through external authority alone, or through objective dispassionate knowledge, our centre of gravity is changing. We are now seeking wisdom, not only through external sources, but through a combination of intuitive knowing and personal experience. No matter how many books we read, or what advice we receive from others, it does not touch us unless something resonates within our own hearts and connects us to consciousness in an authentic way. Therefore, most chapters of this book conclude with an invitation to listen to the Spirit, through meditative silence and through a word from sacred scripture. The short meditations are designed to help you enter into your own heart, trusting the wisdom of the indwelling Spirit. They are not designed to fix or change anything, but to make space for healing and transformation, and more importantly, to make space for seeing more of the miracle in your life, and in yourself.

And so, let us begin again, even if through tired eyes, to rekindle the curiosity and wonder whereby we 'see anew' the glimpses of the Spirit in the miracle of our lives. When we begin to believe something new, we will see something new. We can only discover life's lessons together, for none of us has a monopoly on wisdom; we are interdependent in this adventure, we lead and need each other to acquire collective wisdom. This wisdom does not usually come through loud persuasive voices or dramatic occurrences like earthquakes or storms, but most likely it comes subtly and silently through a gentle breeze – of awareness and invitation. So, let us listen attentively for that gentle breeze where wisdom reveals herself. 'She never fades, by those who love her she is readily seen, by those who seek her she is readily found. She anticipates those who desire her by making her known first' (Wis 6:12).

CHAPTER 1

Inviting the New:
Healing Our Disappointments

*No need to recall the past, no need to think about
what was done before. Look, I am doing something
new, now it emerges; can you not see it?*

ISAIAH 43:18

I t was a beautiful morning in late spring. The sun peered
tentatively through the café window as people chatted over
breakfast or waited for a takeaway coffee. I caught the eye
of an elderly lady sitting at a table opposite me; we smiled
briefly at one another. She looked chirpy as she glanced at her
watch and looked out the window every few minutes,
obviously waiting for someone. Eventually, her friend arrived,
a sad-looking lady with a hardened expression on her face and
a suspicious look in her eye. The chirpy lady welcomed her
with the greeting, 'Beautiful morning, isn't it?', to which her
grumpy friend replied, 'Huh, 'tis fine to say "beautiful
morning", we will pay for this later in the summer. Sure look
at the summer we had last year.' Somehow, that tentative ray of
sun seemed to shyly disappear, the world around me seemed to
lose its beauty, the 'something new' was no longer visible
behind the clouds of cynicism and gloom that emanated from
that table. I wondered how many disappointments and unhealed
hurts had coagulated in this woman's heart to have taken the
light from her eyes and the spring from her step. Perhaps she
was protecting herself from yet more disappointment by closing

that valve of hope in her heart. Perhaps she had good reason to believe that summer will not come into her heart, that it is not worth trusting because people betray you in the end, so why bother, as, in her own words, you 'pay for it later'. Her face held a kind of 'don't come near me' look. Apparently, we can constrict and contract the muscles in our bodies and faces to adapt to our thoughts and our defences through a mechanism of 'body armouring'. This type of defence mechanism is meant to be a temporary state, whereby we ward off potential danger, but sometimes it can become a way of life. Unfortunately, we can become so defensive against life that we shut down the heart and ward off anything that doesn't endorse our cynicism and narrow worldview. When we live and relate from the heart, our energy is warm and inviting, but when we close the heart, we live in fear and suspicion, making everything seem cold. It is difficult to embrace the new, so we sometimes create a comfortable old hammock out of past events and all the old disappointments and injustices. We return to this old hammock with every new challenge or setback.

Gospel stories are full of this tension, that of embracing the new or holding onto the old. When Mary anointed the feet of Jesus, and the room was filled with the beautiful scent, not all could appreciate the fragrance or the beauty of this generous gesture. Some saw it as pure waste, asking, 'Why was this ointment not sold for three hundred denarii and the money given to the poor?' (Jn 12:5).

When the man born blind had his sight restored, some objected because they perceived him as *a sinner since birth*. Jesus himself was criticised for healing on the Sabbath. Likewise, when the women ran from the tomb on Easter Sunday morning with good news, they were considered to be crazy; 'this story of theirs seemed pure nonsense, and they did not believe them' (Lk 24:11).

Wet Blankets

In her book *The Artist's Way*, Julia Cameron uses the term 'wet blankets' for those who put a dampener on the fire of enthusiasm or on the creative dreams in your life. She advises, hold your intention within yourself, stoking it with power – only then will you be able to manifest what you desire. She also suggests, we must move silently among doubters, to voice our plans only among our allies and to name our allies accurately.[4] Jesus tells us to wipe the dust off our feet when we sense we are in a negative environment. Of course, sometimes, it is we ourselves who are the wet blankets, throwing cynicism on a tender dream trying to grow in our own hearts, or in the heart of another.

On an Easter Sunday morning, I was sitting in the garden trying to journal something about resurrection or transformation. I sat with pen and paper but nothing came to mind, no inspiration. I thought of various images of transformation, but still no words came. Disappointed, I was about to give up when suddenly a butterfly landed on my page! I gasped as the little creature moved its wings as if to say, *look, can you not see?* I sat for quite a long time, captured by a sense of wonder, looking and listening to the silence between us. I just gazed at this butterfly and marvelled at how it had once emerged and resurrected from the tomb of its chrysalis.

Filled with an excitement that I imagined Mary must have experienced running from the tomb on Easter Sunday morning, I too wanted to run and tell someone about my butterfly. I ran to tell someone, anyone … but unfortunately chose a wet blanket! My excitement was met with, 'Oh, that was probably an old winter moth; they are around everywhere this time of year, just looking for somewhere to die'!

The critics within and without are always ready to kill the new, to recall the past, to haul it back up and create a backlash against the new deed. The choice to see the world filled with new life and butterflies, or just old winter moths waiting to die, is a defining one.

The call of Isaiah invites us to see anew: 'I am doing a new deed, look, can you see it' (Is 43:18). This is quite a challenge

---

[4] Julia Cameron, *The Artist's Way* (London: MacMillan, 1992), p. 199.

against negativity, both that of our own and others. Familiar pain and belief systems can sometimes feel easier to believe than the new miracle we are being invited into. The chip on the shoulder can start out innocently enough, probably when something tender in us was betrayed – our trust or our hope. This usually happens when we are little and unable to make sense of it. When the betrayal of our trust becomes pushed down out of consciousness, an 'emotional scab' forms over it. The original wound might no longer be visible, but the scab grows and develops into a kind of grudge against life, which builds and attracts cynicism and negativity. The problem is not just what this grudge does to our own hearts and bodies, but how it circulates around us, looking for companions in negativity. It is sad to see someone living a life where butterflies can no longer delight them and summer sun cannot warm their hearts, and where there is nothing new at which to be amazed. When we miss those daily revelations of the Divine, which can change our lives irrevocably, the heart can become embittered. Eventually, we no longer *have* bitterness but we *are* bitterness, we no longer *have* disappointment, we *are* disappointment. Just like the lady in the café, who carried the 'don't come near me' look in her face, we can unconsciously drive away the very thing we are crying out for – someone to see the hurt. Perhaps she longed to be met where she has lived unmet all her life, but I doubt it will happen too easily while she hides her vulnerability behind her hard, scowling armour. According to the law of attraction, like attracts like, and we bring towards us what is uppermost in our minds like a magnet. If that is true, then perhaps while we are focusing forever on what is wrong or negative, then more of it 'shows up'. If that is the case, did the complaining lady attract even more things to complain about … the cold coffee, the delayed service? I don't know how true the whole concept is regarding the law of attraction, but I do know we are called to let go the scab – the 'hard done by' attitude that engenders negativity around us.

The Desire to be Free

We have an innate longing to let go, to be free of the burden of resentment, bitterness and grudges. We have a desire to let go of our limiting, familiar prisons of fear and the patterns that these prisons can create. When we live in fear, we create a world of fear around us, and we lose touch with the things more vital and beautiful within us. Jesus always made contact with this desire in human beings to be free. Something in our souls defies tight definitions and limiting worldviews and longs to be part of something greater and more expansive.

In order to heal and understand our fear, we have to visit our story; we have to understand what we did to receive approval, or what we 'sold out' on to earn our belonging. We need to discover the strategies we employed to survive, and the neurology attached to these strategies. We need to expose the wound, because that wound, paradoxically, can be what keeps our hearts open. The wounds in our lives can be agents of transformation when they place us in kinship with others in compassionate relationships. As Leonard Cohen sings, 'There is a crack in everything/That's how the light gets in.' Our wounds have hidden in them a pearl of great price, they can even contain the 'mustard seed that becomes the greatest of trees, so that the birds of the air come and make nests in its branches' (Mt 13:32).

Growth happens when we are open and self-reflective. Our spirituality must evolve from the conventional level (believing what everyone else believes) to the individual level (standing our ground and our own inner world) and finally to the interdependent stage (knowing our own inner world whilst also connecting with others). Without awareness and self-reflection, we become stuck at one of these stages. We can conform and try to 'blend in' so much that we never develop our own beliefs, or we might assert our individuality so much that we cannot integrate beliefs beyond our own. Likewise, we need to move from the *intrapersonal* (that which resides within ourselves) to the *interpersonal* (what is going on between us) to the *transpersonal* (the mystery that transcends us). When we touch the vast mystery of what it is that lies beyond us, we are touching the 'more than' and the reality of a collective unconscious. We are all made for this expansion; we are designed for broader and more creative horizons, and for the natural evolutionary process of our psyche, both individually and collectively. For this growth to evolve, we have to confront our conditional and limiting images of self, life and God. Our fear and rigidity is softened when we discover and grow into the wonderful truth of knowing who we are, and whose we are. When air and light can get to the wounds that have never been seen (even by ourselves), we finally begin to come home and our projections fall away. We begin to let go of some of the old, tired ways of seeing life (where nothing surprises us anymore and we react to everything in the same habitual way). Paradoxically, when we begin to 'own' our pain, we make space for something new; we make space for joy. As Kahlil Gibran reminds us, 'Your joy is your sorrow unmasked. And the self-same well from which your laughter rises was oftentimes filled with your tears.'[5]

Reflection

Give yourself a few moments of silence. Allow your mind to fall still. Simply relax, don't try to get rid of anything – just be present. Allow your body to become comfortable and bring a gentle awareness to your breathing. Feel, without judgement, where your body feels tight, constricted, defensive. Breathe into this constriction and gently let surface an awareness of where and how you hold this armouring in your life. What does it feel like? What is it saying? Does it manifest as a kind of grudge against life, or a fear around your ability to trust? If so, do not judge yourself for this. Do not try to change anything or make yourself feel differently. Allow yourself to feel surrounded by the warm rays of Divine light enveloping your whole body, touching especially the places that are hard

---

[5] Kahlil Gibran, *The Prophet* (London: William Heinemann, 1980), p. 36.

or cold. Rest and breathe in this light. Allow the armouring to be softened, visualise your heart being connected with, and healed.

CHAPTER 2

Seeing Through Specks: Restoring Our Sight, Recovering Our Truth

I care not what others think of what I do, but I care very much about what I think of what I do. That is character.

THEODORE ROOSEVELT

Two disciples were on their way to Emmaus. They walked along in a downcast mood, their faces etched with disappointment. They shared their story with someone who joined them on the road, someone who drew them out when he asked, 'What matters are you discussing?' (Lk 24:17) He invited them to share their disappointment and he walked with them while they told their story. When the story was told they recognised him, and their eyes were opened. They knew then that they were in Divine presence and their hearts were burning within them.

Sometimes we have to acknowledge our own broken dreams. Only then can our eyes be opened; otherwise, like the disciples, something prevents us from seeing. The psalmists don't hold back when it comes to lamenting their downcast emotions. Psalm 22 reads, 'My God, my God, why hast thou forsaken me?' (the same sentiments that Jesus recalled in his moment of agony on the cross). Sometimes our spirituality requires that we name and lament our own shattered dreams and experiences, otherwise the memory of these experiences block and cloud how we see everyone and everything. When we unmask our own hurts, we no longer need to have 'hate figures' to project onto, and we tend to lessen our blaming of circumstances. In fact, we embrace the wounded in both ourselves and others. It is difficult to invite the poor, the blind and the lame in the way the gospel asks of us, if we have never met the poor, blind or lame within ourselves. Most of the time, we hardly notice that something is preventing us from seeing or preventing us from living in the present moment, and therefore we are seldom without the luggage of yesterday or the fear of tomorrow. Consequently, we are often only partially seeing ourselves or others – our prejudices and transferences (the outdated maps whereby we bring an old story and project it onto a present-day one) are getting in the way. Therefore, when we notice that there is a lot of 'heat' in an argument, or we are having a strong reaction towards somebody, it might help to ask 'Who am I really seeing here?' Sometimes the reactions we are experiencing may not be related to the person in front of us, but are in fact belonging to a previous relationship where there is still some unfinished business.

A Dam Holding Back a River

Our perceptions get clouded over by residual issues from previous experiences and relationships, which form a template and eventually become woven into our identity. Our energy and life force can also be inhibited, when we repress unwanted energies. This repression can feel like a dam holding back a river, and a river longs to flow! When part of our energy is blocked, our 'sight' gets limited and eventually we may settle for a distorted psychological worldview.

We can get so used to this limitation, we just put up with it, and consequently can suffer an on-going, low-grade depression, whereby experiences that fit into our fearful inner world are accepted, and those that might challenge or contradict them are rejected. We then subconsciously limit our capacity for happiness. Even though we might experience an absence of any real inner joy, we can get so used to feeling dissatisfied we have normalised it. Like the sound of air conditioning, we get so used to it we don't even notice it is there, yet when it stops we discover a new stillness, one we have never really experienced before. Unfortunately many of us just plod along and manage to survive in this half-alive type of existence until, over time, we resign ourselves to remaining happily miserable! But we are designed for more than just managing to survive; we are created to be fully awake, fully alive; we are made for greatness, to feel the fire burning in our hearts. There are tiny epiphanies in our everyday lives reminding us of this – if only we could see.

'We see things not as they are but as we are'

I can now see the truth of something once said to me: 'We see things not as they are, but as we are.' As I sit here, leg elevated, nursing torn foot ligaments, I see not people but feet. I never had any previous interest in shoes or feet. Now I don't see faces but feet everywhere. I wonder how comfortable people's shoes might be, I notice how lean their feet look, how perfect their toes seem compared to my own purple swollen ones. It is said that when the pickpocket meets the saint, he only sees his pockets. When the beatitudes ask us to be 'pure in heart', they ask us to face each moment and see each experience and person with fresh, new eyes, and with undivided, non-biased presence, so that when we ask how someone is, we are asking for them, not for ourselves. In this purity of heart, we are appreciating the person for the gift that they are, not as our expectations or agendas would want them to be.

Taking the Log from the Eye

A log in the eye creates specks everywhere, we are told by Jesus, who cautions us: 'Why do you observe the splinter in your brother's eye and never notice the great log in your own?' (Mt 7:3). When we are looking at the world through specks, we are projecting something from the log in our own eye. We hook our stuff somewhere, we repress or we transfer it, we deny it or disassociate ourselves from it.

Early childhood hurts can become lodged within, encoded at a cellular level. A child longs to have his/her soul mirrored, its very existence is given through the affirming mirroring of an adult. When reassurance or affirmation is withheld at some stage, the child might stay emotionally stuck at that age. Later in life, though the person may forge a wonderful career and achieve great things, an emptiness lurks inside. Eventually it becomes exhausting trying to build compensatory devices to get our mirroring and affirmation from success, achievements or the applause of the world.

We all have self-doubt to varying degrees, but when we exaggerate one dimension of our lives to compensate for a perceived, or real inadequacy, we live with the incessant anxiety that we might someday be 'found out'. 'How am I doing?' becomes the persistent question torturing us from within. This question and the insatiable needs of the insecure self become the primary motivation, rather than the intrinsic value of whatever, or whomever, we might be engaged with at any given time. Right now, I can think of little else other than the pain in my injured toe. It is similar when our self-worth has been injured – we can think of nothing else other than that pain, and how this person, project or possession might soothe it. We can, out of this unconscious longing for approval, seek positions where people soothe our egos, respect us, look up to us or need us.

Allowing Ourselves to be Found

Our 'persona', as psychologist Carl Jung called it, is built to compensate, but we can hide behind it. The persona or 'adapted self' is the mask we wear for the world, and is often designed to create an impression. We care very much what others think of what we do, we are fed by outside validation and held up by the scaffolding of how others perceive us, as well as by mood-altering positions of power, status and achievements. 'What then will anyone gain by winning the whole world and forfeiting his life?' (Mt 16:26). We can indeed win the world, yet still feel like nothing is enough, that it never really nourishes or soothes our thirst; it feeds the ego but starves the soul. Like drinking salt water, we get even thirstier after each drink. Perhaps that is why, when Jesus met the woman of Samaria, he offered her a spring welling up inside, an eternal spring that would soothe her thirst and nourish her from within, bringing her home to her true self. This spring wells up inside of us too, when we remove some of the debris and obstacles that block its flow and allow ourselves to be encountered. Jesus was searching for the woman more than she was searching for him. Likewise, God searches for us, and desires to find us and free us from the hiding place of the false self. Sometimes we can put the emphasis on our own efforts, in us finding God. I think it is more the other way round – God is finding us. The expression 'finding the Lord' has always irked me, maybe because I don't think I ever found the Lord, but thankfully, despite all my hiding, God has managed to find me.

Finding the Lord

There is a story of a drunk man who, coming out of a pub late one night, hears the sound of singing down by the lake. Excited at the idea of a party, he staggers down to join them. They are an evangelical group performing a 'born again' ritual, whereby each person is immersed into the water as the others recite prayers for this person to find the Lord. The drunken man volunteers to be immersed into the water. When he comes up, they ask, 'Well son, have you found the Lord?' 'No,' he replies, in a slurred and confused voice, so they drop him in again and they repeat, 'Sir, have you found the Lord?' 'No,' he replies again, and so a third time: 'Have you found the Lord? 'No,' he answers impatiently, 'I haven't found him … are you sure it was here that he fell in?'

God is forever searching to find us, even while we are looking somewhere else and not wishing to be found. Sometimes we are afraid that we will, in our shame, be 'found out' – and so we hide behind our defences, our roles and even our religion. When Jesus joined the disciples on the road, he allowed them to find him at the breaking of bread. He allowed himself to be found by a woman at a well. Likewise, divine love is seeking to find us – on the road, at the well, in the kitchen, in the office, coming out of the pub. We just need to allow ourselves to be found.

Reflection

Take some time to relax, to slow the breathing and to allow the mind to fall still. Each time an urgent thought or emotion comes, acknowledge it, but try not to hold onto it. Become aware, without judgement, of how you hide – from others, from yourself. What do you avoid seeing in yourself? How do you project it outwards? What 'specks' (faults) do you repeatedly see around you? What log may be causing this blurred vision? Allow Jesus to walk along the road with you for a while, showing you where your eyes may need to be opened, where you need to see anew. Try not to 'do' anything, just listen. Allow yourself to be still, and in the stillness allow yourself to be 'found'.

CHAPTER 3

The Road to Hell:
Letting Go of the False Self

*One of the symptoms of an approaching breakdown is
the belief that one's work is terribly important!*

BERTRAND RUSSELL

P ublic humiliation is the stuff of nightmares. It was
Good Friday night. I was facilitating a prayer
experience around the cross in a parish church. I had
worked so hard to ensure it was well prepared, believing of
course that my work was terribly important. I had written
some short reflections and Taizé chants, all interweaving. I was
doing it all by myself (rather like the single grain of wheat in
John 12:24: 'Unless a grain of wheat falls to the ground and
dies, it remains a single grain'). I wanted my presentation to
be beautiful, perfect, impressive. I said a quick prayer
beforehand (hoping that God would find it impressive too, I
suppose). This was in the time of cassette tapes and tape
recorders, so I asked the altar server to be ready to insert the
tape when he received the nod from me (it was a tape I had
made myself, with the Taizé chant 'Stay Here and Keep Watch'
on one side, and some songs I'd recorded off the radio on the
other). I welcomed the crowd, read the opening prayer, invited
people to sit back and to listen carefully to the words of the
music … and then came the defining moment: having nodded
to the server, he inserted the tape, pressed 'play' and over the

sound system came Chris Rea singing, 'This is the road to hell'. Oh no, wrong side of the tape! Red-faced and weak-limbed, I crossed the sanctuary to turn off the tape. I apologised profusely, a few at the back walked out, the others smiled and made whispers to one another. For one attached to self-image, it sure felt like 'the road to hell'. In hindsight though, maybe Good Friday was a good day for the grain of wheat to fall.

Blindness of the False Self

The false self tends to conceal those parts of the personality that seem unacceptable to the outer world. These parts get pushed away and become what Jung refers to as our 'shadow'. We reject those aspects of ourselves that do not seem to comply with the outer image we want to portray. This might mean we hide our anger, jealousy, our failure or traits we would insist are 'out of character' for us. The shadow often reveals itself through dreams, through other people's feedback (which might not always be positive), through unexpected mistakes (like the Good Friday experience), or through bodily symptoms. Jung cautions us that the less we own the shadow, the blacker it becomes. The good news is that apparently when the shadow is brought into the light of awareness and integrated, it is 90 per cent gold, because it leads to fuller integration and growth.

Sometimes we only recognise there is something wrong when we discover our life lacks lustre, when we are sick and tired of being sick and tired! Our life may seem perfectly calm on the outside, whilst inside we feel like we are walking on stilts. When we scratch below the surface, we meet the anxiety and the fear that nearly always lurks behind the false self and its associated defensive energy. The needs of the ego are often at variance with the depths of our being, which is why the mystics and spiritual writers have so much to say about ego defences being something we must wrestle with on our spiritual journey: 'It is our false selves which see ourselves as potential subjects for special and unique experiences.'[6] However, we can be consoled that Jesus smiles patiently as he sees us make that journey, for he patiently accompanied his disciples, who right up to his death argued about who was the greatest. The ego self must die so that the beautiful self we are meant to be can blossom and bear fruit. The defensive dynamics of the false self – where we are always in charge, never wrong and always doing it 'all by ourselves' – can feel imprisoning for our spirit. It can feel like 'the road to hell'.

Displacement of the ego can create access to our deeper being; maybe the ability to laugh at ourselves helps this process along. At such times, we can discover a mystery larger than the confines of the self. Maybe we are thrown into transpersonal landscapes, the ones the mystics and the prophets inhabited, when the bottom falls out of our little world and we lose something of our attachment to self-image. As Patrick Kavanagh suggests in 'From Failure Up', 'when we are faced downwards with our noses in the rubble that was our achievement' and that often it is from down there that we are most receptive to 'the music playing behind the door of despair'. Wouldn't it be wonderful if our crumbling institutions could hear that music playing as they lie with faces downwards and their noses in the rubble of what seemed like achievements? Kavanagh's poem tells us that something beautiful can grow out of this place.

> Can a man grow from the dead clod of failure
> Some consoling flower
> Something humble as a dandelion or a daisy,
> Something to wear as a buttonhole in Heaven?
> Under the flat, flat grief of defeat maybe
> Hope is a seed.
> Maybe this's what he was born for, this hour
> Of hopelessness.
> Maybe it is here he must search
> In this hell of unfaith

---

[6] Finley, *Merton's Palace of Nowhere,* p. 81.

Where no one has a purpose.
Where the web of Meaning is broken threads
And one man looks at another in fear.
O God, can a man find You when he lies with his face
    downwards
And his nose in the rubble that was his achievement?
Is the music playing behind the door of despair?
O God give us purpose.

Reflection
Come to a place of quiet, return awareness to your body and
your breathing. Again, without judgement, focus your
awareness on the energy you invest in your achievements and
your attachment to your role in life. What do you gain? When
do you over-invest? What do you often feel you have to
defend, protect (your good name, self-image, position in work
or community)? What does this defensiveness do to your body,
your emotions and your spirit? Can you bring this awareness
and associated tiredness into the compassionate embrace of
God, allowing yourself to drop the burden, even for just a few
minutes?

CHAPTER 4

Revealed to Mere Children: Rekindling the Wonder of Childlike Wisdom

Every child is an artist. The problem is how to remain an artist once he grows up.

PABLO PICASSO

We are to welcome the kingdom of God like a child, Jesus tells us. He rebukes the disciples for preventing the children from coming forward – for it is to them that the kingdom belongs (Lk 18:16). It seems that the natural dispositions of a child are good for receiving what God wants to give us: trust, present-moment living, sense of wonder, play, spontaneity – characteristics of the self that knows itself to be one with God. Thérèse of Lisieux formed much of her spirituality around the concept of spiritual childhood, doing by grace what a child does by nature. She discovered a profound relationship with God through her childlike trust.

An elderly man recalled with me a summer night in his childhood when he stayed out late playing football with his brother. Delighted at all the goals he had scored, he rushed in home in great spontaneity to tell his mother about his wonderful triumph. 'I won, I won!' he cried, only to be met with, 'Look at the state of your clothes!' His bubble of excitement was burst, and his enthusiasm was dampened and somewhat shamed. These and many other innocent, yet shaming, reprimands over the years gradually chipped away at his sense of wonder and ability to be amazed at himself and at his life. He grew up cautious, suspicious of emotion, and prided himself on how sparing he had become with spontaneity and anything that he considered to be foolish. Later, he reflected on how so much of his life and many of his choices had been made out of this curbed enthusiasm; in fact he felt he had made a career out of it – he became a philosopher, admired for his carefully thought-out and often muted responses and his discerning prudence. He did, however, have regrets, some of them relating to how he had sometimes restrained some of his students' spontaneity and had over-emphasised reason and caution to them.

Undoubtedly, this man had lived a good, dutiful life. He never did 'foolish' things and examined everything carefully before making decisions. But something was missing. He remembered sadly the words of love he could never let himself utter to somebody he had cared for deeply. He had once given her a rose but never asked her the question that he so much wanted to ask. He never knew, and she never knew, what asking that question might have meant. He lamented the many times he was afraid to say 'yes' to life, or 'yes' to love. He said he felt like the rich young man of the gospel – obedient and dutiful all of his life, but with the unlived life catching up with him. He felt afraid to live and afraid to die. He was a spiritual man but now felt, as divine love looked upon him, that he needed to let go of that which he had protected so carefully all his life. It was hard to let go of the 'possessions' he had grown to trust, which included his guarded privacy, always being right, being the type of person that people looked up to. Behind the veneer of perfect poise there lay a hidden grief. He had intellectualised and institutionalised the spirit of the child.

It was through a crisis, a type of breakdown, that he finally began to search for the spontaneity and aliveness he had left behind. He found it difficult to share his grief with me, as he did not like giving up his resilient self-image and the sense of control he had grown to depend on. He nearly 'went away sad' (Mt 19:22), but thankfully he stayed with the journey, where he sensed what he described as 'divine love gazing upon him steadily'. Thomas Merton, contemplative mystic, tells us that one glance of divine love, and the false self could dissolve. The elderly man stayed with this divine glance long enough to discover his deeper worth and his spontaneous self beyond the 'riches' he had come to depend on. In fact, one day not so long ago, I happened to drive past him and I saw him making his way down the hill – where, to my astonishment, he seemed, at moments, to be actually skipping. He didn't see me, but I silently celebrated the moment – the child was back.

Rules that Restrict

We pick up rules from our caregivers, our school system and religion. Some are good, necessary and life-giving, but we must continually ask ourselves what we are to leave behind and what we are to take with us, reflecting like the householder who brings out from his storeroom new things as well as old (Mt 13:52). Otherwise these internal rules can set up residence inside us, picking away at our humanity and spontaneity. It is exhausting (for others as well as ourselves) when we feel we have to be always right and always sensible. When we let go some of this defensiveness, we get back a lot of our energy and vitality. We might consider our need to be right or sensible 'our religious duty', but Jesus always challenged and discerned what might be empty observances from what constitutes authentic spirituality. Healthy religious service creates a joyful sense of contribution, but internalised rules, beliefs and habits can create neurosis and make for an unlived life. Fear-based adherence to the law inhibits the unfolding of the real self, as the song 'The Rose' reminds us:

It's the heart afraid of breaking that never learns to dance.
It's the dream afraid of waking that never takes the chance.
It's the one who won't be taken who cannot seem to give.
And the soul afraid of dying that never seems to live.

There's a story of a little girl asking her mother on Christmas Eve why she is cutting off the end of the turkey before putting it in the oven. Her mother tells her, 'Because my mother always did it'. The little girl rings her granny to ask why *she* always cut the end from the turkey, who replies, 'Because my mother always did it'. So the little girl asks her great-grandmother. 'Because,' her great-grandmother replies, 'I didn't have an oven big enough to fit a whole turkey!'

We often cling to old, unexamined and tarnished blueprints, simply because they are established. Sometimes they do not bring life and have nothing to do with real spirituality; they suffocate our spirits and make religion seem stuffy and lifeless. Let us remember again the child you and I once were, and remember what amazed us before we started worrying about what everyone else thought of us. There is a strong link between innocent wonder and healthy spirituality. I am reminded of this every time I meet Buttons, who loves everyone, irrespective of whether they like her or not. Buttons is a puppy who specialises in hospitality. Whenever there is someone to welcome or someone that needs comforting, she goes towards them immediately, which often results in her falling down the stairs, off the sides of armchairs, or foolishly running across the road – risking everything just to be with you. Buttons is no respecter of our to-do lists, no respecter of status, achievements, or of the world's wisdom. She shines her love on the just and the unjust alike. Animals are like children: they bring us all to our innocence, where the only thing that matters is that we love one another, and of course that we play. They remind us that there are things hidden from the wise and clever but revealed to the little ones. In their company we feel young, whether we are eight or eighty. Maybe this eternal youthfulness, this honest trust, even that which appears foolish, is what is celebrated in eternity.

Reflection

Come to the quiet centre again. Allow your body to become comfortable and your breathing to be free and natural. Ask the Spirit to reveal what blocks your sense of wonder. Become aware of the internal 'rules' that often inhibit your spontaneity – 'you must not, you ought not, it's not proper to …' Whose voices are these? When you follow them, whose life are you living? When did you internalise them? What do they do to your spirit? Are they in alignment with the Spirit of God who reminds you, through Jesus, that he came that you may have life? What did you love to do as a child? Why did you stop doing these things? When did you lose your sense of play? If you were less concerned about being sensible, what would you try again today? Bring this discernment to the Holy Spirit and ask to be shown what rules you can leave behind, and what you will take with you.

CHAPTER 5

What If ...:
Letting Go of Anxiety

Yahweh is near to the broken-hearted, he helps those whose spirit is crushed.

PSALM 34:18

I lost a relic. Someone told me it was a mortal sin, but if you did your level best to find it and told it in confession, you would be forgiven. But now St Martin de Porres was gone and it was my fault. I stayed off school the next day and the day after, frantically looking for him in every drawer of every cupboard as I repeatedly asked myself, 'What if I haven't tried my best to find him?' If I stopped looking for a minute I feared that I was in danger of committing the dreaded mortal sin. The fact that I was called after him didn't help my plea when I earnestly, but with confusion, asked him to find himself! No sign of him, time for confession and to get whatever sentence I would receive over with. Terrified, I blurted out to the priest, 'Bless me Father, I lost St Martin.' No answer. I tried again, a bit louder this time, 'I lost St Martin and I don't know if I did my best to find him.' Still no answer. My mind started racing with all sorts of catastrophic thinking. Oh God, maybe he knows the other stuff I have done too. I'd better say it. I took a deep breath and decided I would get it all said in one sentence: 'And Father, I think I might have meant to kill my sister when I threw her off the load of bales.' Still no answer, just a deep sigh. That sounded serious, but I decided I'd better keep going now anyway. 'Also Father, I let the Holy Communion touch my teeth by mistake. I stole a Black Jack ... ' The priest stayed silent. He seemed concerned (which I interpreted as him pondering on which of my sins were mortal and which were venial). I was *definitely* going to hell, I thought to myself, that place where I would be forever and ever, all on my own. The only consolation was that I had heard somewhere that animals didn't go to heaven, so at least I would probably have Nipper, my Jack Russell terrier, there with me in hell. I burst into tears and sobbed uncontrollably. The priest asked me if I was OK, he reassured me that I was not going to hell and questioned whether I wanted to talk to him when he was finished with the other confessions. I said, 'There's no need, Father, but do I need to go back and pay for the Black Jack? And must I come back again if I don't find St Martin?' I was seven years old, and I did come back. I came back many times, often repeating the same 'sin' and checking if something was mortal or venial. I was suffering the torture of the nameless 'what ifs' ... what if I'm damned forever, alone, bad, going to hell? Each night I feared I would do something, or think something and the trapdoor would open and down I would go – forever – and Nipper and I would never be seen again! Each night I said my prayers, trying not to look at the statues and their disapproving faces (even those whose heads had fallen off seemed to be talking about me), reminding me that I had fallen short again today. As for St Martin, I prayed to St Anthony that I would find him, but I never did.

Nameless Dreads

A child's world can be dominated by what psychoanalyst Wilfred Ruprecht Bion calls 'nameless dreads'. These dreads need to be soothed and held by our primary caregivers. As children, we needed an adult to supply a 'container', to soak and absorb our fears, and to give us back the message, verbal or otherwise, that we are safe and the world is a safe place. But if the parent themselves is anxious, fragile or fearful, they may not be able to offer us this container; in fact, we can end up reversing roles and absorbing the parent's fears. These 'floating fears' can fill us with existential dread. The endless 'what ifs' can permeate every cell in our bodies and we can carry this type of anxiety into adult life. These fears are usually unspecific – we hardly know what we are really worried about, and in fact sometimes we worry that we are not worried! A client of mine once shared that her waking thought each day is, 'Now what is it I'm supposed to be worried about today?' She identified with this internal state of anxiety that robbed her heart of any real relaxation. Patterns of anxious thinking, worry and fear can, over time, become habitual – we fear rejection, abandonment, humiliation, annihilation and loss. It helps to understand where these fears come from and to compassionately consider how lack of a secure base in childhood plays havoc with our sense of safety and ability to relax. While patterns of worry, anxiety and nameless dreads are not easy to let go of, we can, over time, allow a healing of those memories. But we also have to be resilient and committed to new beliefs, new ways of thinking and behavioural action, lest we slump back into familiar fear-filled, self-defeating habits. Most people have insecurities and fears to some degree, but if they are excessive, they may have roots in childhood 'nameless dreads'.

Abandonment Fears

There were green cards on the table, one for each animal being sold that day in the mart. The cattle truck would come to collect them on Tuesday mornings. A cousin from Dublin was there that morning, he looked at the green cards and said, 'Oh look, there's one here for Martina today.' Everyone laughed, but I didn't. My heart was beating wildly. I panicked, thinking that maybe the moment had finally arrived, the one I had always feared: what if they really did want to get rid of me; what if I was not wanted; what if I really was a burden, what if … Now the hour had come. I was going to be sold, sent off. The lorry came and went and I was not collected – what relief

– but the next Monday night and many Monday nights following, the familiar dread started in my stomach. The clock seemed to tick very loudly, as loud as my fearful heart. I would sit alone in the kitchen, listening to the far distant sound of the milking machine from the cow stall, where my mother was working. The yellow of the walls sickened me, as I tried to tell myself that there was still a chance I might not be sold. Finally, the tension of not knowing became too much. I went out in the dark night to find my mother and ask her the dreaded question. I waded through the muck in the rain and stood behind her, asking the question, as I stared at her raincoat: 'Mam, am I going to be sold?' She didn't turn around but simply said 'Ah don't be silly, go in out of the rain, put on the kettle, I'll be in soon.' The 'what ifs' and the ticking of the clock didn't seem so loud now.

Compassion for the Child

Our abandonment fears can create persistent worry in our life and in our relationships. We can remain forever vigilant for signs, perceived or real, of abandonment. We can cling to situations and people that are not good for us because we are so afraid to leave, or be left alone. We can even do the abandoning first as a kind of 'getting it over with', before someone abandons us. More seriously, we often abandon ourselves. The first step towards healing is to see with compassion the little person we once were and what we did to survive, what we did to try to 'make people stay', or how we tried to keep our world safe. When we understand how we tried to control the uncontrollable (where no one dies and no one leaves us), we begin to soften towards ourselves. Eventually, we need to practice trust and surrender in place of worry and fear. This is like strengthening an unused or limp muscle – it has to be exercised and strengthened regularly. We need to find an inner sanctuary in place of outward certainties. We need to access our adult selves in order to gently parent the frightened child of our hearts – that little person that still lives inside of us. It is not too late to take care of that frightened child, to promise that we will never abandon that fearful part of us, but will create safety and compassionate presence so the 'what ifs' can be soothed.

Reflection

Come into stillness within yourself and allow your mind to fall quiet and your breathing to relax. Bring your awareness to your body, and any anxiety that seems to lodge there. Bring awareness to any places you seem to feel fear or anxiety ... tummy, throat, chest area, neck or shoulders. If any of these parts had a voice, what might they say? Perhaps try saying a few sentences: 'I am afraid that ... ' What age is this person who is afraid? What are the 'what ifs' that still play in the background of your life? Imagine your adult self now beginning to take care of this little fearful part. 'Let the little ones come; do not stop them,' Jesus says. Imagine the little one in your heart spilling out the fears and all the 'what ifs' and see yourself surrounded by the unconditional love of God and the love of your own heart.

CHAPTER 6

Satin Cushions:
Allowing Ourselves to
Enjoy Life

I shall give you a new heart and put a new spirit in you.
EZEKIEL 36:26

———————————

'Thank God we got the hay saved before the rain,' I used to hear them say. What do you mean 'thank God'? I wanted to shout. If God is getting the praise, he needs to take the blame too! He should say sorry for all the suffering my father is going through, lying in a hospital bed covered in plaster from his neck right down to his hips. I only heard pieces of what was happening … a rare blood disease … a form of cancer … softened bones … serious neck operation. But still, I joined in when we all said 'thank God'. Thank God he lived as long as he did – seven years he lasted. Deep down I didn't want to thank God for all this suffering; I didn't want to thank God that I lived in what a school friend later described as 'the house that always had the ambulances calling'. 'Offer it up' were words I often heard. I didn't want to offer anything up, I just wanted not to watch my mother silently cry, not to watch her get sick from the worry of it all. I wanted my father to be like other fathers – at home with us. I wanted to be able to tell my mother about things that had happened at school, or things I was worried about. I wanted my father to be proud of me when I finally learned how to turn the hay without breaking it up. I wanted to have the freedom to sing out of tune and still feel I brought him joy. Just for one day I wanted not to feel sorry for him. I wanted to feel what it might be like not to tiptoe around so as not to disturb him. I wanted to laugh out loud just occasionally and not feel I was stealing a bit of his happiness. And still I was to say 'thank God' – not from a grateful heart, but from a place of resigned hopelessness, an offering up of your lot. I watched my mother struggling with the secret of my father's illness all on her own. She told no one how serious it was, but kept it bottled up, alongside the reality of her own repeated illnesses.

My father was a man of the land. He loved every field, every ditch, every briar and every hawthorn bush. I have memories of him stepping back to admire something as simple as a briar that he had just cut back, or an old ditch he had managed to rebuild. He respected nature and treated it with gentleness and care; seemed at his happiest when he was gazing at a ploughed field, a budding tree or the wood he had cut for the fire. But now he was torn away from the land that he loved and was surrounded by tubes and machines. He was torn away from the place of his soul. His despair was palpable to us even as children, so we dared not make it worse by anything we would say in his presence. Instead we censored our words, and always added 'thank God!'

The medical chart hung at the end of the bed. I tried not to look at it – the graph on it frightened me, because I imagined it had written on it how long he had left to live. At the end of each Sunday visit, I would feel so guilty for abandoning him in a place where I thought he was being punished for something. I couldn't look at his suffering face and, most of all, at his aloneness. I tried not to look back each time we left the hospital. I think I felt guilty that I had the freedom to leave and he didn't. We sometimes stopped at the corner shop and the shopkeeper would give us a fist of satin cushions – those coloured sweets with the lovely creamy chocolate in the middle. One Sunday after leaving the hospital, I had a lovely pink and green striped satin cushion in my mouth, and then I thought: 'I cannot enjoy this sweet while Dada is suffering in there.' It felt somehow disloyal to enjoy anything, so I removed the satin cushion and held it in my hand for the rest of the journey home. Every trip in that Morris Minor was accompanied by my mother repeatedly singing, 'Cruising Down the River' in an attempt to lift us out of the sadness. However I had already made up my mind that life was no cruise; rather it was hard, cruel and to be endured. When my father died, I unconsciously vowed to remain loyal to his memory by never exceeding his own level of happiness and staying forever true to this inheritance of sorrow.

Not until much later in life did I realise I was living a script my father would not want for me. I sensed he was now set free of all that bound him – the tubes, machines, tablets and plaster, the depression. Today, whitethorn bushes remind me of him, and when they blossom they seem to whisper: *live your life, live it fully, honour those gone before you by living your life.* Somehow the man of the land seems to ask me now and then to buy a fistful of satin cushions and maybe even say 'thank God' as I bite right into the creamy chocolate centre.

Letting go our Loyalty to Sorrow

Sometimes we make unconscious vows based on family sorrow. Somehow we imagine we are being loyal to those who suffered by embracing all the sorrow we can endure; perhaps we might even go looking for hardship. Worse, we feel guilty if something good comes into our lives, and feelings of being undeserving can cause us to subconsciously limit our capacity to receive good things. We may push them away, or we may sabotage them in some indirect way. All of this is very subtle. *Who would go looking for suffering?* I hear you say, but if we carry an inner belief system that *this is what we deserve,* or this is *what our family deserves,* we may make choices accordingly.

I worked with a young woman in therapy who had survived a very painful childhood of repeated abuse and violence. She continued to choose abusive partners and seemed to have no interest in stable, secure men. She met a lovely man who adored her but she 'felt bored' and finished the relationship. She had felt bored because she missed that adrenaline of living on the edge, the drama of never being sure, of having to chase men, fight them, and in so doing continue the dysfunction she was used to. She stayed in toxic, disrespectful and abusive relationships; she didn't trust kindness, affirmation or compliments, and taught herself to always expect the worst so she wouldn't be disappointed again. However, she had a beautiful soul and I knew that one day she would come home to herself and discover who she really was, and what her heart truly longed for and deserved. Recently, the man she previously found to be 'boring' came back into her life, and they are getting married. The boredom issue seems to have disappeared, maybe because she has stopped running after shadows and feels less guilty about letting go of her need to suffer, and is finally allowing herself to receive respect, love and care in her life. Perhaps she is finally allowing herself the 'satin cushions' of life. As Rumi, the Sufi poet, reminds us:

> Come, come whoever you are.
> Wanderer, worshipper, lover of leaving, it doesn't matter,
> Ours is not a caravan of despair.
> Come, even if you have broken your vow a hundred times,
> Come, come again, come.[7]

Reflection

Allow yourself to settle into a quiet space. Be attentive to the beating of your heart and the pulse of life within you. Be aware of the Spirit breathing life into you at this moment, at every moment. The Giver of Life wants to offer life to you, wants to prepare a banquet before you, life in all its fullness. How do you limit yourself from receiving? What holds you back? Notice the scripts you carry with you about 'not deserving', or the blind loyalty you may have to some family sorrow.

---

[7] Jelaluddin Rumi, as quoted in Sy Safransky, *Sunbeams: A Book of Quotations* (Berkeley, CA: The Sun Publishing Company, 1990), p. 67.

Visualise yourself letting go of this legacy from the past, knowing that those who have gone before you are not asking you to suffer in this way. Begin to say a conscious 'yes' to all that God delights in giving to you.

CHAPTER 7

Moving On:
To Transfer or Transform?

You became an actor, instead of a reactor, a player in the game of life rather than a spectator watching from the sidelines while life passes you by.[8]

With excruciating detail, we remember the pain — the look, the word, the silence — that wounded our heart. 'I never look back,' an acquaintance proudly said one day, 'the past is the past, and we have to move on.' As she continued her point, she held her fists tightly and her lips were pursed. 'We hold our issues in our tissues,' someone once told me. Somehow I didn't feel I wanted to tell her about the parts of my life that I am unable to 'move on' from just yet.

Society places a high value on moving on. When somebody hurts us, we are sometimes advised to move on; when a career, relationship or dream gets shattered, we are told to move on. Sometimes we think that moving away or moving on is how we relieve ourselves of the pain, but often the opposite is what we need to do. When we visit the places of our wounding, we also, paradoxically, visit the places of our healing. We need to stay with and sit with our pain, because the medicine is often in the wound. When we connect with our vulnerability, we

---

[8] Sidney B. Simon and Suzanne Simon, *Forgiveness: How to Make Peace With Your Past and Get On With Your Life* (New York: Warner, 1991), p. 182.

can connect with our inner life, where our gifts of intuition, perception and, most of all, our compassion reside. It is compassion that heals, and that draws us into solidarity with others who have also known the pain of being human. All the great stories and myths have at their core the journey of transcending suffering and pain, the 'coming through' being what builds character.

Mythologist Joseph Campbell, author of *The Hero With a Thousand Faces*, tells us that when we embark on a journey, we are initiated into a fuller life through embracing our suffering. Heroes are those who transform and transcend their suffering, not those who simply 'move on'. Childhood pain can indeed embitter us, but it can also set us on a journey of asking the big questions: *what is my life all about, what meaning does suffering have, where is beauty, what is it that endures?* These questions are spiritual questions, but they sometimes need to be preceded by a letting go of the 'why' questions: *why me, why him, why not her?* We may need to move on from some of the 'who did what to whom' questions, like those asked of Jesus, in trying to root out who exactly is to blame. 'Rabbi, who sinned, this man or his parents that he should have been born blind (Jn 9:2). The 'who caused it' questions may be necessary, but rarely bring true healing. In asking these types of questions, we may find the answers we seek, yet continue to carry the full weight of the pain.

Through my work I once crossed paths with a man whom I admired greatly; he was an open-hearted person, full of fun, but what I admired most about him was the way he was with his children. He seemed to always have his car full of his own and neighbours' kids, and they were invariably heading off to a match somewhere. One day I mentioned to him how great he was with his kids. He stopped and reflected, and then said wistfully, 'I suppose I'm that way because of my father.' He then went on to say that his father was an alcoholic, and sometimes violent, and he remembered how he used to long for his father to accompany him to matches and other places, but he was never there for him. Because of his painful childhood memories he had vowed to always be there for his own kids.

This man also has a relative who drinks heavily, and when he gets drunk he becomes aggressive and argumentative, and absent to his children. When people ask him why he is always so angry, he too says, 'I'm that way because of my father'. These two men both had similar childhood experiences. They both moved on, but in different ways. One passed on a blessing from the pain of the past, the other merely passed on the pain.

Reflection

Allow yourself to relax and become aware of an area of your life or a situation from which others, or yourself, have been advising you to move on. Perhaps you have been investing a lot of energy in trying to force yourself to rise above it. Maybe you feel stuck in the 'who did what to whom' questions. Can you surrender these questions a little and surrender the compulsion to move on. Maybe it is enough to befriend the wound. There may be a gift in the pain for you or maybe a blessing for others can arise out of your pain as you move on.

CHAPTER 8

Best in Class:
Letting Go of Our Need
to be Perfect

I myself stand in need of the arms of my own kindness –
I am the enemy to be loved.[9]

CARL JUNG

How we earned our worth and how we got our sense of belonging were powerful forces in our early lives. What we developed to get the attention we longed for and what we did to stay out of trouble shapes much of our behaviour today. As children we were amazingly skilled at adapting to what we thought was expected of us, even if it was never verbalised.

When John came for therapy, he was suffering from fatigue; his life had been shaped by a desperate attempt to gain his father's approval (who had died many years earlier). He could not get off the treadmill of having to prove himself, first to his father and later to all authority figures. He gave up on his dreams to gain this approval. He squeezed himself into a career that was totally incongruent with his values, and aborted his dream to become an artist. He had learned to say yes when his body and soul were trying to say no. He had learned to scan every changing temperature in his emotional environment so that he could fit into what he thought was expected of him.

---

[9] Carl Jung, *Modern Man in Search of a Soul* (New York: Harvest/HBJ Books, 1933), p. 235.

In so doing, his true self went underground. He was brilliant in his career, but empty in his life.

It is common to hear words like 'well done, top marks' offered to children for achieving, but what happens to our sense of worth the day we don't get top marks? What happens when our identity gets fused with achievement, or 'being good', or intelligent, or whatever it is that we are praised for? When this over-identification with what we do occurs, the bar gets raised higher and higher and nothing is enough. When failure is very hard to face, perfectionism becomes the driving force of our lives − a treadmill difficult to get off.

When I was younger, I always felt relief when the bell went and we'd have to return to class after break. I hated playtime. I was always afraid in the playground. I felt stupid and inferior. I couldn't let myself play just for the sake of playing − what if I got it wrong and they laughed? Then I would feel even more ashamed. Deep down I was jealous. I longed to be spontaneous, free − to just be one of the gang. This sense of separateness was paralysing. I felt I could not let go and row in on the rough and tumble like the others. (I think I must have learned somewhere that playing was silly, and so I discovered instead how to talk about sensible, adult things.) The words of a poem by Stephen Spender, which I learnt in school, stay indelibly in my mind:

> My parents kept me from children who were rough
> Who threw words like stones and who wore torn clothes.
> Their thighs showed through rags. They ran in the street.
> And climbed cliffs and stripped by the country streams.[10]

It was the closing lines of that poem that impacted the most: 'They threw mud/And I looked another way, pretending to smile,/I longed to forgive them, yet they never smiled.' I still shudder at those words, as does anybody who remembers what it was like to be on the outside, secretly longing to be included,

---

[10] Stephen Spender, 'My Parents Kept Me From Children Who Were Rough', *New Collected Poems* (London: Faber & Faber, 2004), p. 110.

but too frightened of 'the bullies', whilst covering the fear by pretending to smile.

I felt great security when we all went back into class, my comfort zone, especially if it was English class, where I was 'elevated' from my shame, and where I knew I would get praise. I might even be told again today that I was 'best in class' (which gave me a secretive feeling of superiority). Here I knew I was 'somebody', I was good at something and I was less afraid of those 'who threw words like stones'. I took in the teacher's affirmation like a drug – needing more and more of it. I sat up near the teacher and looked at her as she looked at me (or so I imagined). I tried to be the good girl, always giving the right answer. I was her right-hand girl, forever trying to make her proud of me, and that became my criteria for feeling worthy. I laughed at her jokes, even if they weren't funny. I tried to become everything she could want me to be. My happiness was in her hands. Then came the day I could not thread my needle in sewing class. I asked my friend to do it for me, and then told the teacher I had done it myself! She got very cross and scolded me for lying. I did not feel perfect or special anymore; the teacher did not seem perfect or special anymore either – and I did not want to sit near her again. I felt ashamed in front of the other children, and so all the feelings of inferiority and stupidity returned – I was no longer 'best in class' and anything less than that was useless!

On the Outside, Looking In

It is paralysing when we always have to get it right, when we have to be the best, the most special. Perfectionism has nothing to do with getting it right. It has nothing to do with fixing things. It has nothing to do with standards. Perfectionism is a refusal to let yourself move ahead. It is a loop – an obsessive, debilitating closed system.[11] Our longing to feel 'part of' and connected is often in conflict with our need to feel special and unique. I thought 'being the best' and excelling was what

---

[11] Julia Cameron, *The Artist's Way* (London: MacMillan Publishers Ltd, 1992), p. 119.

would make people proud of me. If I got a cold, or fell and cut myself in the playground, I feared I would be a burden, so I learnt to be perfect in an attempt to feel loved. However, keeping a safe distance in the playground of life is a lonely place – where we do not run in the streets lest we fall or get dirty, feeling like spectators, always on the outside looking in. We might live like spectators forever and never know why we feel this way. We might construct ivory towers where real life cannot touch us. We might later learn how to hide behind respectable roles, careers, convents, monasteries or academic institutions. Perhaps we become specialists or consultants, offering great advice to the world. We might engage in charity work, throwing coins to a beggar but never seeing his face, praying 'over people' but never asking them for prayer for ourselves.

When we cling to anything that elevates us above our humanity, we break a vital link with ourselves and with others. Our inferiority and superiority are just opposite symptoms coming from the same wound. When we try to make ourselves special or different, we isolate ourselves, we add more suffering to our pain. However, we discover, in our falling and our rising, that 'we are so intimately joined in Divine Mystery that when a single one of us falls, we are all wounded. And when a single one breathes freely and opens to the exquisitely painful ecstasy of love, we are all nourished.'[12] Real healing brings us back into the circle of humanity. Sometimes, the pendulum may swing too far towards the need to be independent where we say *I'll do it myself, I'll look after myself, I'll be resilient*. In psychological terms, we might mistakenly call this the 'individuation process'. Certainly, if we have been over-dependent on others, we have to move towards autonomy, developing a sense of self and therefore moving towards a more independent stage. But it must not stop there – we are intrinsically interdependent. No matter what stories we tell

---

[12] Gerald G. May, *Will and Spirit: A Contemplative Psychology* (San Francisco: HarperOne, 1987), p. 321.

ourselves about our illusory separateness, we are intimately connected with others. We expand through engaging in a sense of 'we' and not just 'I', 'for in the realm of contemplative quiet, beyond all ideas, beyond our rainbowed images of God and self, beyond belief, we share the same silence. We are rooted all together in the ground of consciousness that is God's gift to us all.'[13]

Perhaps on those days when we are unable to pass through the eye of the needle on our own, and we are 'found out', some of life's lessons become illuminated. When we lose the privileged position of sitting next to the teacher, we are thrown back into a more liberating place. The mother of James and John discovered this too when she also wanted her two sons to sit near the teacher: 'Promise that these two sons of mine may sit one at your right and the other at your left in the kingdom' (Mt 20:21). The mother of James and John was advised by Jesus not to look for privileged places, but to follow his example in drinking the cup of suffering; the cup of life, to do as he himself did, seeking not to be served but to serve.

We discover who we are not when we are the best in class, or the worst, but when we allow ourselves to feel our belonging to the family of humanity. We are advised not to seek such places where we must always be first or the most important, but to consider that often it is the first who in fact are last, and those considered last who are the first. Therefore, let us be content on those days when we know we are not the best or not the worst, but when we know we are all equal in the playground of life – and we are all beginners.

Reflection

Bring yourself into a quiet place of remembering. See yourself as a child again. What did you do to gain the approval of authority figures (parents, teachers)? What did you develop to stay out of trouble? How did you make yourself shine? What did you get praised for or what did you feel you were admired

---

[13] Ibid., p. 319.

for? How did this make you feel? How did you hide, become a spectator? What part of yourself did you 'sell out' on? What did you try to get rid of in order to be liked? How did you earn your place then? How do you do it now?

Simply welcome this awareness without analysis, allow the split-off part of yourself to return for healing and integration. What may seem to have been unworthy of love may be the very part of you where God desires to meet you.

CHAPTER 9

Keeping the Door Open:
Forgiveness

Love your enemies and pray for those who persecute you.
MATTHEW 5:44

We all agree on how important forgiveness is – until we have been hurt. 'You must forgive' are easy words to preach until we experience what it is like to have our souls betrayed and our trust violated. Seventy times seven, Jesus tells us, is how often we need to be able to forgive. Perhaps when saying this, he knew that as soon as we would forgive, we would bring the old injury back up and replay it, not seven times but seventy times seven.

I got a nasty text once. It was late at night. I read it and felt shocked at first, but then reflected on how much life had hurt this person and how tortured she was. I knew her hurt had caused her to create hate figures, and now I was one of them. Somehow, I found it within myself to light a candle for her and sent her blessings from the depths of my heart. Or so I thought. The following morning I was driving to work and reflecting on the words of the text. I felt my grip on the steering wheel grow tighter and my foot increase pressure on the accelerator. I became lost in a world of imaginary ways of getting my own back. 'I'll show her, how dare she,' I muttered, until I noticed I was over the speed limit. 'Seventy times seven' the Spirit seemed to remind me, and I remembered lighting that candle the night before, which had seemed so easy then but impossible now. 'Resentment is like taking poison and hoping the other person is suffering,' someone once told me. The only person suffering that morning was me, so I relaxed my clenched grip on the steering wheel and eased my foot off the accelerator.

Of course, we are not meant to negate our own hurt, pain and anger, but sometimes (as in the above example) we need to be 'big enough' to see beyond, to be able to let go, to shake it off, and not allow something to hold us captive. I knew when I received that text initially that it was important not to give it power and not to take it as necessarily meaning something about myself as a person, but rather to look at it as a symptom of the hurt and pain that the sender was in at that time.

Any healthy practice of spirituality points to forgiveness as being integral to inner peace. It can take a long time, and maybe all we can do is try to keep the heart and the door open towards resolution. *Bless her and change me,* my mother advised me to pray whenever someone would hurt me. Hey, steady on – that's asking too much. I can only sometimes get as far as change her, make her see how much she hurt me and make her change her ways, and don't forget to bless me for all the ways in which I've been hurt. I think God likes honest prayers (even those ones where we unknowingly pray that our forgiveness includes us winning the battle). God knows what we are made of, and somehow in the fullness of time, in *kairos* (an ancient Greek word meaning an opportune moment or the 'right' time), our hearts can be transformed, or the door to resolution can open. I don't think forgiveness is something we do; I think we can only let it be done unto us or through us. Our frightened hearts find it very difficult to forgive, but something happens when the hurt that we find unmanageable is handed over to a higher power.

Keeping the Door Open for *Kairos*

My mother left a very good example of keeping the door open. A relative of ours had closed himself off from all the family, refused to speak to any of us, and locked himself away in a world where he needed no one. He turned up at funerals but never engaged with anyone. After many years he became the family member no one ever mentioned anymore, except to occasionally pass on the story of his existence and lament how he had turned his back on everyone. My mother, however, carried him in her heart to daily Eucharist for over twenty years. She prayed for him each day. Quietly, she visualised him sitting next to her in the chapel seat receiving the blessings she was sending him. One day, there was a knock at the door at home and there he was, hand in a sling, crying, 'I have cancer and I don't know where to go.' She opened the door wide and asked no questions. She arranged to have his luggage collected the next day and nursed him until his death. In the weeks leading up to his death, this proud man who had needed no one could not let her out of his sight. He cried whenever she left the bedside, his worn, wrinkled face now irrigated by a lifetime of unshed tears. He had become a child again, trying to be reborn, and my mother was the midwife who prepared him to meet his own heart so that he could meet the heart of God. He died surrounded by her love, and somehow I think, because someone on earth had kept the door open, he was able to recognise love again when the door of eternity opened and his tear-filled face met the tear-filled face of Christ.

Reflection

Maybe there is an unfinished story in your life, someone who did not keep the door open for you but rather walked away. That is the worst – when we are left without a voice. Try not to let it define you, or to allow it to eat into your self-esteem in a way that erodes your trust in yourself or in others. Visualise yourself handing this hurt (and the person who hurt you) over to God, as you understand God. In scripture, we are promised that our prayers do not come back empty: 'It will not return to me unfulfilled or before having carried out my good pleasure and having achieved what it was sent to do' (Is 55:11).

You are not denying your anger and your sense of loss, but you are asking for it to be carried (and for yourself to be carried). You are trusting that someday the door may be opened, or you are asking for wisdom, or to simply have the strength to let go. Perhaps you might need to ask for courage to say what has not been said, or for guidance to know the wise thing to do. Perhaps you can say 'Bless them and change me', but if that feels too difficult, simply breathe and rest in the God who sees you, loves you and holds this dilemma with you, and helps you to say:

> God grant me the serenity to accept the things I cannot change,
> Courage to change the things I can
> and the wisdom to know the difference.[14]

---

[14] Reinhold Niebuhr, 'Serenity Prayer'.

CHAPTER 10

Hidden in the Bag:
The Judging Mind

The weapon, with which we would destroy the enemy,
must pass through our own heart to reach them.[15]

THOMAS MERTON

It was a Saturday afternoon. The crowds watched from a distance as a middle-aged lady was led through the shop by a security man and a guard. One of them spoke into a mobile phone as the lady plodded along, face downcast, clutching the bag with the stolen clothes. Some of the bystanders tut-tutted as she passed by. I looked at them, noticing how well-dressed they were. I looked at her, and I wondered who those stolen clothes were for, and why she was coming out of the children's department. I wondered what life had dealt her, and why she had to steal a few children's clothes. Her own clothes were shabby and wrinkled. It wasn't the guard or the security man I felt anger towards, it was the women who cast glances as she passed by. 'Disgrace,' one of them muttered. 'She got what she deserved,' added the other. 'God forbid that we all get what we deserve,' I said under my breath, but when one of them looked at me, I quickly added, 'There but for the grace of God go I.' One of the ladies, on hearing me, quickly replied, 'You don't steal, do you?' I didn't answer out loud, but

---

[15] Quoted in Wayne Muller, *Legacy of the Heart: The Spiritual Advantages of a Painful Childhood* (New York: Simon & Schuster, 1993).

thought of all the ways we can steal. We steal people's good name, we steal another's dignity, we steal the joy from others, we steal too much of the world's riches, we steal opportunities. We are just lucky we are not found out most of the time, and so avoid 'getting what we deserve'.

Later that evening I prayed for the lady who stole the clothes. I tried to pray for the women bystanders also, but somehow it didn't flow as freely. I don't fully know why I felt so angry with those women – perhaps I feared their self-righteous glances and how they would consider me to be a 'disgrace' also if they found out all I carried in the bag of my life. I don't know what the guards said to her – maybe they compassionately led her to hand back the clothes, and maybe she was handed back her dignity, and that somehow through the experience she heard in her heart 'neither do I condemn you, go and sin no more'. Maybe she was, after that day, one of those who 'forgave much because much had been forgiven her'. They are all just maybes, but I hope that our ways are not God's ways and that someday she might be the one to lead me – and the judgemental women – to be with him in paradise.

Judging Eyes

Judging eyes can be very harmful towards ourselves and towards others. They dissect and divide and miss the full spectrum of the story, instead building our case as to why *I* am right and *you* are wrong. When we have judgement towards another, we look at them with hard eyes and ruthlessly seek out what is wrong, incorrect or missing, and judge what we see. Sometimes we can preach about morality or justice as something hard and legal, an 'eye for an eye' approach. When have you endorsed that type of seeing? Can you recognise the one you are judging to be your brother or sister? We often hear of the need to see the beauty around us and to know it is within us, but do we not also need to see that the 'sin' around us is also within? The Buddhists take a vow of non-harming towards self and all creation; we would do well to follow their example here. Jesus advises 'judge not and you will not be judged'. We are advised not to pull at the weeds of our heart, or the heart of another, for in doing so we may pull up the wheat also. Rainer Maria Rilke puts it another way: when we get rid of the demons, the angels might go also. When we judge ourselves, we may set up a civil war inside our own being – two parts of the self divided against each other. It is not easy to give up our judging mind. Sigmund Freud coined the phrase 'superego' to describe that incessant internal critic from which we must hide all our failings and weaknesses from its vicious attacks. It is part of the structure of our psyche that tries to control our 'id impulses' (instincts, drives etc.). The superego is the moralising (and punishing) voice in us that tries to ensure we fit into socially acceptable behaviour and cultural norms.

Facilitating a group of teenagers in recovery once, I asked them to try to abstain from judging themselves for one week and to observe any differences in their level of peace. At the end of the week one of them said, 'I really missed my critic, I had become used to living with it, and found it hard to let go.' It can be difficult to let go the habit of self-criticism and criticism of others, especially when we have normalised it. But when we let go a little and begin to see ourselves and others with softer eyes, we see not just the faults and failings, we often see how that person is perhaps doing the best they can. We see a bigger picture, and in seeing with softer eyes we can say, 'there but for the grace …'

Reflection

Can you look with softer eyes at the wheat and the darnel in your own heart, the beauty, goodness and kindness you give to others, alongside the ways you steal beauty, goodness and kindness from others? Come to the quiet place, begin to visualise yourself holding the light and shadow, the wheat and darnel of your life and your heart, with tenderness and compassion. Allow yourself to be looked upon with tenderness by the one who sees even that which you have 'hidden in the bag'. Divine Love might be inviting you to hand over the bag of your possessions, all that you are grasping so tightly – not to judge or count how much you have hidden there, but simply so that in dropping the bag, your arms are free to receive the arms of Divine Love.

CHAPTER 11

Croissants in Paris:
Receiving Abundance

Though you have no money, come! Buy and eat;
come; buy wine and milk without money, free!

ISAIAH 55:1

They had told me about the art, the wine, the romance, the ambiance, but they never told me about the croissants! In our guesthouse we had tea, coffee and that awful milk but, ah, the croissants. I had a great idea: I would keep some of them from breakfast and pack them into my bag with some butter, and carry them with me, and I could have them later on. I walked around the Champs-Élysées and Montmartre, tired from the heat, but postponing my much-anticipated croissants. I prided myself on holding out, delaying gratification for another while, until finally I reckoned I had earned one. I succumbed to the moment I had longed for all day. I stopped at a café, ordered coffee, and when the waitress wasn't looking I sneaked the croissants out of my bag. Yuck! They were squashed and flattened and there was butter everywhere! As the waitress arrived with the coffee, I began trying to take the money from my greasy, butter-stained purse, when I noticed that with the coffee she was handing me a plate of croissants! I protested, fearing how much they would cost. 'Oh no, I didn't order them,' I insisted. She smiled knowingly and said, '*Madam, ils viennent avec le café gratuit*'!

Hadn't I once heard something about heeding the birds of the air and how they do not 'gather into barns but their Heavenly Father feeds them' (Mt 6:26)? Apparently, when the Hebrews were on the way to the Promised Land, God fed them manna, but they were not supposed to store it overnight. They were to trust that God would supply new bread the next day. Trusting in Providence is a disposition of the heart, a way of knowing that we will be looked after, that we do not have to store up, earn, beg or 'butter up' the Giver of the free gift. Likewise, we don't have to store up prayers and good works to earn our eternal paradise in the next world; in fact, a little bit of Paradise is being offered right now. It might be offered to us in a form we don't expect, such as a card in the post, the sound of the breeze through the trees, someone making you a cup of tea, a lovely sunset, a pet delighted to see you. Little glimpses of paradise are all around us – if we can open our eyes and notice. 'Now it emerges, can you see it?' (Is 43:18).

My bag would have been lighter that day if I had believed what the mystics and enlightened ones had told us: that Divine Providence can only gift us when we are empty enough to receive. But when we hoard, gather into barns and store up things, we block the flow. Our fear of deprivation and scarcity is often behind our need to store up as much as we can. But storing up will not heal our fears. It takes a lot of energy to defend what we have in storage, when we feel like everyone is a threat; they could take the few croissants we have! But when we live trusting that each day is a gift to be lived fully, and when we trust we have enough and we are enough, our cup overflows. When we have trust, simplicity and expectancy, 'more will be given, but he that hath not, even what he hath will be taken' (Mt 13:12). If we lived today with gratitude and with a sense of abundance, we would echo something of the piece entitled 'If I Had My Life to Live Over', written by Erma Bombeck after she had been diagnosed with a fatal illness:

I would have talked less and listened more. I would have invited friends over to dinner even if the carpet was stained and the sofa faded. I would have eaten the popcorn in the 'good' living room and worried much less about the dirt when someone wanted to light a fire in the fireplace. I would have listened to my grandfather ramble on about his youth. I would have never insisted the car windows be rolled up on a summer day because my hair had just been teased and sprayed. I would have burned the pink candle sculpted like a rose before it melted in storage.[16]

Reflection

If you had your life to live over, what would you do less of? What, or with whom would you invest more time? What would you consider to be essential? What would be the non-essentials, those you could let go of? What would you do today if it was your last day on earth?

---

[16] Erma Bombeck, *Eat Less Cottage Cheese and More Ice Cream: Thoughts on Life from Erma Bombeck* (Kansas City, MO.: Andrews McMeel Publishing, 2003).

CHAPTER 12

Out of the Silence:
Restoring Our Centre of Gravity

*We can make our minds so like still water that beings
gather about us, that they may see, it may be, their
own images, and so live for a moment with clearer,
perhaps even a fiercer life because of our quiet.*[17]

W. B. YEATS

O ne eye on the clock, my day planned: glad that last
meeting went so well, a quick coffee, pop into the
chapel, and then off I go. They say if you want to
make God laugh, tell him your plans. Not sure God was
laughing that morning, but my plans were certainly altered for
the next eight weeks. I tumbled down some steps and went
over on my ankle. What is it about falling that makes us feel so
foolish? I pretended to smile as I picked myself up, and tried
to walk again, looking around, hoping there was nobody
watching.

Eight weeks later my foot was still up, and there was not
much sign of the ankle improving. 'God's way of slowing you
down,' numerous people said. Dubious theology, I thought –
I doubt a sinister God planned to make me fall to teach me a
lesson. However, we can find meaning in setbacks, and God
can draw us into deeper stillness when we are not running
around 'playing God'. I rang some work colleagues to see how
they were getting on (expecting that the place had fallen down

---

[17] W. B. Yeats, 'Earth, Fire and Water', from *The Celtic Twilight: Faerie and Folklore*
(1902) (Minole, NY: Dover Publishing, 2011) p. 69.

without me), and to my surprise the world was continuing to turn quite well in my absence. A valuable lesson: 'Thank you, God, for reminding me yet again that I am not the one who makes the sun shine every morning!' Initially, frustration kicked in and I fought against this enforced rest; it felt like one of those places the gospel reminds us 'we would rather not go' (Jn 21:18). Eventually, I surrendered. Perhaps it is time to listen again, to see again the world that is always offering itself in new ways to us, if we can let go of control and the busyness that chokes off our inner receptivity.

Resting in God

Resting in God restores our centre of gravity and empowers us to do God's work. It alerts us to when we ourselves have 'become God of the work' rather than the other way around. It re-establishes our centre of gravity so we can say *I can do all things through Christ who rests in me*. It gives us a childlike lightness, which reminds us that we are part of the dance, but we do not control the dance: 'When the world meets people whose centre of gravity is within their authentic selves, it draws close to them like moths to a magnet.'[18] But it is one thing to be free of external pressures; it is more difficult to be free of internal ones – those that drive you from within, those that tell you to keep pushing, proving, competing and producing. We become afraid that if we stop we might lose our place, our purpose and our position – all those things the ego equates with life itself. In the silence we discover those attachments that are diminishing us and blinding us from the real longings of our souls.

One of my favourite passages in scripture is from Mark's Gospel, describing Jesus heading off for morning meditation: 'Before dawn, he left the house and went by himself to a lonely place where he could be by himself' (1:35). If Jesus needed to do this, we certainly do also. Perhaps that is why he was so

---

[18] Daniel O'Leary, *Unmasking God: Revealing God in the Ordinary* (Dublin: Columba Press, 2012), p. 55.

focused, able to say things like, 'My food is to do the will of the One who sent me' (Jn 4:34). Can we as clearly say what our food is, what energises and motivates us? It was out of this contemplative dimension that he strongly advised Martha to slow down, to sit still, so that in that stillness she would drop some of the feverish running around and discover 'the one thing necessary'. Jesus also encouraged his disciples to rest: 'Come away by yourselves and rest for a while' (Mk 6:31). He asked them to do what he himself did, even in the busiest times, when he was most in demand for miracles and preaching. Maybe that is why he was able to say, 'No one takes my life from me, I lay it down of my own free will, and as I have power to lay it down, so I have power to take it up again' (Jn 10:18). Everyone can take our life from us when we lose our own centre; in fact, we hand over control of our lives when we look outside for our identity. When we lose touch with the indwelling Spirit as our source of life, we run the danger of expecting others to be the source, in other words, to be like gods for us. We can become co-dependent on others when we expect them to be gods or when they expect us to be gods for them, and in asking from them what exceeds their humanity, they will probably run in the opposite direction.

The Body and Resting

We have been given a wonderful inbuilt mechanism for dealing with emergencies through the sympathetic nervous system. Through the fight or flight response, we have an ability to speed up all our faculties – heartbeat, concentration, brain signals – as adrenaline is pumped through the body. If, for example, you are driving your car and suddenly someone runs across the road in front of you, you have an instant response whereby all your faculties kick in and you can act with amazing alertness. When the sympathetic nervous system is switched on like this, another system is switched off in us – the parasympathetic nervous system, which concerns itself with digestion, production of enzymes and other things (the flow in the body). As wonderful as all this is, we need to remind ourselves that this alertness and pumping of adrenaline is meant to be temporary, it is not meant to become a way of life. So while it is unlikely that someone will run across the road in front of us every day, or unlikely that we have daily critical experiences, it can feel like the daily demands of life become one emergency after another. If this is the case, we will be drawing on the adrenal glands too much and could run the possibility of adrenal burnout. This adrenal burnout may develop from continuous stress in our lives. Depending on our psychological make-up, on-going conflict, anxieties and fears may be keeping us in that persistent fight or flight mode. It is not so much the actual external stressor that is significant, rather it is more the impact it is having on the body and our response to it that makes something stressful. Therefore, if there is conflict or tension in your relationship, or if you are consistently afraid of someone, or being controlled by someone, you need to be aware of what is happening in the body. But it is not just the negatives that drain our adrenal glands; the seeming positives do also, whereby we may be pushing too far in our competitive goals, for example in work – straining after promotions, adhering to tight schedules, meeting targets and so on. We need to create a way of life that is a buffer to such stresses and gives regular relief to the sympathetic nervous system. We need to cultivate nourishing friendships, time with nature, time in solitude as well as in creative pursuits – times where we respond to the invitation to come away and rest for a while.

Scripture tells us that those who take time to wait on God will 'rise up like eagles, they will run and not grow weary' (Is 40:29). This seeming paradox – where resting brings speed – is interesting. Somebody once asked a guru how long he meditated each day. The guru said, 'I usually meditate for thirty minutes, except when I'm very busy – then I meditate for sixty minutes.' We search and wait for a hidden treasure through the practice of relaxation, but like scripture reminds us, we may have to sell the field to receive this treasure. We may have to sell the notion that *the world depends on me* and that *if I do not do it, nobody will.* We may have to sell what we own – the strategies we employ to keep the outer show on the road (while ignoring the inner longings for rest). We may have to sell the notion that a quick coffee and a 'pop into the chapel' can sustain us for the day! Silence and meditation are necessary in our lives if we are to avoid the kind of burnout that results from pushing too hard: 'Be still; listen to the stones of the wall. Be silent, they try to speak your name. Listen to the living walls. Who are you? Who are you?'[19]

Reflection

What stops you from resting? Where is silence in your life these days? Be aware of the ways you might avoid silence – those times you tend to stay pushing, proving yourself or talking because you fear silence; maybe you fear you might hear something beneath the chatter of the mind. This can feel threatening initially, but if you stay with it, you might hear the still small voice of your own soul. You might discover a glimpse of who you truly are, you might hear your name being called, and for the first time recognise that your name is written in eternity.

---

[19] Thomas Merton, *The Collected Poems of Thomas Merton* (New York: New Directions, 1977), p. 280.

CHAPTER 13

Contemplation:
A Way of Seeing

Make your home in me as I make mine in you. As a branch cannot bear fruit all by itself, but must remain part of the vine, neither can you unless you remain in me.

JOHN 15:10

Nothing around me is new and yet today everything is new – the birds have not stopped singing since I injured my ankle, and somehow it is only now I really hear them. Those brazen rabbits I previously considered a nuisance are now thrilling me with their playful frolics as they happily nibble at my flowers and shrubs! Even the crows, whose cawing usually irritates me, are today welcomed into this banquet called life. A group of swallows pass overhead, I look up at them and at the same time I notice a blackbird on the branch that is also looking up at the swallows. We are sharing the same vision, breathing in the same air; we are in the same moment. When the swallows have passed over, there is a silence again. The blackbird tilts his head as if he is looking at me, I am looking at him, and we are sharing the same silence. This silence is not just an absence of words; it is the presence of something else. I dare not put a name on the something else, except to say it feels like being part of something expansive, vast, where we are all one and where nothingness feels like fullness – a fullness beyond measure. This must be what the mystics referred to as mystical consciousness. Tomorrow, I suspect there will be nothing more than annoying crows and burdensome rabbits, but today, I am seeing anew.

This type of seeing where everything is illuminated in an interconnected oneness occurs when we are silent and attentive. It is sometimes called contemplative seeing, and while central to the writings of our mystics, it is available to and experienced by all of us. We cannot control or make it happen. In fact, the following evening, I went back to the same seat by the window and waited for the blackbird, and whilst the blackbird did come, I did not experience the same silence or the same beauty as the previous evening. I began to learn that such moments are pure gift – perhaps they are a foretaste of eternal life, whereby we are liberated from attachment to our habitual and surface ways of seeing. We discover there are other ways of experiencing life other than through reason or logic. In this cosmic holistic vision there is a sense of the oneness of all creation, and a sense that something or someone holds and breathes life into all of us, and it is in that breath of life that 'we live and move and have our being' (Acts 17:28).

Too Beautiful to Die

Thomas Merton glimpsed the oneness of everyone and everything in a shopping centre in Louisville one ordinary day. As he watched people passing, 'it was as if I suddenly saw the secret beauty of their hearts where neither sin nor desire nor self-knowledge can reach, the core of their reality, the person that each one is in God's eyes'.[20] He goes on to suggest that if we saw ourselves and others in this way, there would be no more war or cruelty, we would 'fall down and worship each other'. Merton recognised that there is a timeless core within each of us, which he says is like a beautiful immortal diamond, the part of us which is too beautiful to die, and has the face of God reflected in its image. This immortal diamond is probably what we call our soul, the glory of God in us; 'it is like a pure

---

[20] Thomas Merton, *Conjectures of a Guilty Bystander* (New York: Doubleday, 1968), p. 158.

diamond, blazing with the invisible light of heaven. It is in everybody, and if we could see it we would see these billions of points of light coming together in the face and blaze of a sun that would make all the darkness and cruelty of life vanish completely.'[21]

Resting in God, in contemplative prayer, is different to thinking about God. The problem with merely thinking about God is that a thought cannot hold the immensity of a mystery, and so when the thought about God is gone, God is gone also. The vastness and beauty and immensity of God is inaccessible to the analysing mind, it has to be experienced through an inner awakening or received through an inner conversion. Looking at a sunset and receiving its beauty is different to merely thinking about a sunset. Somehow, we sense a presence of something 'more than' when we enter into a deep silence and stillness, but the mystics warn us that the God we think we can understand or fathom is not God. I think we can say that about another person also – we cannot ever understand or know someone fully, there is always mystery and we can only reverence that mystery. Thinking about life is very different to experiencing life. Contemplative prayer calls us to rest in a deep unitive silence where we discover not an analytical understanding of God, but rather an experience and an awakening of what is already there – our oneness with God and our oneness with the sacred in everyone and everything around us. 'To contemplate is to consider something or someone fully, deeply – so deeply, in fact, that we cannot encounter the truth of them, that we perceive a whiff of the sacred emanating from them.'[22] In stillness, we rest in the source of absolute love – that which transcends all our experiences of both the joy and limitations of relative love. When we open the depths of our being to this vast mystery, where time and place disappear, we discover that all of life is touched by the finger of the Divine. Earth is abundant and

---

[21] Ibid.
[22] Suzanne M. Buckley, *Sacred is the Call: Formation and Transformation in Spiritual Direction Programs* (New York: Crossroad, 2005), p. 34.

fruitful because of its innate ability to absorb and receive light and rain; likewise, we need to absorb and receive the presence and energy of the Divine in silence. When we look at nature we see how the energy pulsates through the grass, the flowers and the trees as they grow in silence. We discover, also in that silence, our oneness with God, and though we are the creatures and God is the Creator, we are one. The branch is not the vine, yet is part of the vine. When we see only the branch, and disconnect it from the vine, it is like ego consciousness, but in mystical consciousness we see the whole – the branch, the vine, the roots, we see ourselves interconnected with everything that lives and breathes. We discover this mystery, not through willpower or effort, but through surrender to a love that is beyond us, yet within us. This surrender can feel as if we are passing over a threshold, like crossing the Red Sea, when we let go into a more expansive consciousness. We can feel like an old way of being is now dying (through a type of mystical death), where we die to old dualistic ways, and all our old illusions of separateness. When this happens, we begin to notice the impermanence of everything, ego begins to fade a little, we worry less about the non-essentials, our 'appetite' changes whereby we crave fewer stimulants and seek more solitude, and we awaken to that which is too beautiful to die.

Coming Home

In silence, we hear the words addressed to us to make our home in this vast abundant supply, the source from which we 'bear fruit in plenty'. Living in God and God living in us is what we discover in contemplative prayer, 'with me in them and you in me, may they be so perfected in unity that the world will recognise that it was you who sent me' (Jn 17:21).

Contemplative seeing calls us to a broader consciousness and awareness that every day mystery is unfolding, and that life's lessons are all around us. Jesus could see the Divine in a grain of wheat or a field of lilies. To follow the soul's path does not mean we bypass the body, or see it as an impediment, but it is to recognise that while we are our bodies, we are also more than that; just like the branch is more than a branch of the vine – it is the vine. We have, in the depths of our being, an eternal deathless nature, and when we tune into this energy, it empowers and strengthens us: 'you thus become aware that strength comes from beyond yourself, is greater than you and contains you. Yet it is your strength.'[23] When we discover glimpses of the impermanence of everything, we experience moments where it seems as if time and space disappear, and we sense how very thin the veil is between this world and the eternal one. Of course the self that relies on its own autonomy (the vine cut off from the branch) defies this, and resists what it cannot control, it resists leaving behind old dualistic comparisons between what is holy or unholy. Because of this tension within us, we often feel frozen between two worlds, between the certainties of the old and the risks of the new. None of this is accessible through logic or reasoning. It is more about a silent, receptive receiving of a gift with the awe and wonder of a child. Thérèse of Lisieux advises that knowledge cannot reveal mystery – one has to be little in spirit, whereby we let go all effort and simply allow the Spirit to unfold in us and through us.

In contemplative seeing, we do not try to get rid of anything, we simply cease from over-identifying with thoughts, images and feelings. We then discover a deeper essence untouched by the dramas in our minds and in our lives. We sometimes need to allow even comforting images of God to be taken away so that we experience what Jesus tells the disciples in John's Gospel: that it is to our advantage that he goes away: 'Still, I am telling you the truth; it is for your own good that I am going, because unless I go, the Paraclete will not come to you' (Jn 16:7). This solitude can feel like nothingness, darkness – but it is a darkness in which God holds us safely and tenderly. When the mind becomes still, a sense of separateness dissolves and we discover that what we were so desperately seeking outside ourselves was already within, waiting for us to come home.

---

[23] John Main, *Word Made Flesh* (London: Canterbury Press, 2009), p. 17.

Lord, That We May See

Oh, that we may see the miracle hidden in the things that seem like obstacles on the path. When we slow down we may discover that they, in fact, *are* the path. Meditation, contemplation, stillness and prayer are often adhered to as a kind of quick ritual so we can produce even more, be more effective, be more successful. On the opening night of a six-week course on meditation and contemplation, a new participant asked me, 'What measurable results can I expect to see after doing the six weeks?' He must have felt the results were not measurable enough – he didn't return after that night! 'Measurable results' can be the language of a consumerist spirituality, wherein lies a notion that meditation is the thing that will improve your concentration, circulation, lower cholesterol, blood pressure. This indeed is true, but contemplative practice and most forms of Christian meditation are more essentially about the transcending of the ego self, and more ideally concerned with self-surrender than self-fulfilment. Meditation and contemplative prayer can lead us beyond our own little world, to connect deeply with something pulsating in the heart of all of us, 'like a harmonic that sounds within and brings us into a harmonious unity with the whole of creation, within and without … [A]s each of us comes closer to Christ the whole fabric of human consciousness is knit more closely together.'[24]

Praying Hard

We long to collapse from our fatigued selves onto God's heart, but while we may long for this rest, we also sometimes resist it. Sometimes we pray whilst avoiding 'eye contact' with God. Somebody once said to me that her faith was very important to her; she said, 'I pray hard every day.' I wondered what it is like for God when we are 'praying hard', when we roll up our sleeves, put on our prayer aprons and start giving God orders to clean up the mess of the world: *Come down here, change him,*

---

[24] Ibid., p. 16.

heal her, answer my petitions. This 'praying hard' is exhausting. After a while on the spiritual journey most of us discover that our way of praying changes, that there is less 'praying hard' and more silence. We begin to move from a Kataphatic way (employing use of images, words, stories) to the Apophatic way (involving more silence, listening, waiting, just being in God's presence). We begin to discover that we can live a continuous life of prayer, a praying without ceasing: 'Pray constantly: and for all things give thanks' (1 Thess 5:17). This is simply a way of being, and a way of seeing in the ordinary events of our lives, practicing a contemplative presence whereby we 'approach every encounter, every activity, every meeting from a contemplative stance, trusting God is already at work in people's lives, listening to the Holy Spirit, to others and to ourselves, watching for signs of God's grace, paying attention to every experience, and exploring our sense of God's presence and the shape of God's invitation to growth.'[25]

It can be difficult to embrace the contemplative way. Most difficult of all, we might have to 'sell what we own' – our certainties, our fixed images, our righteousness and our belief that we can earn love by our own efforts. But it is only when we have no handlebars to hold onto, and when we have thrown away the balance sheet and measuring tape of our lives, that we can truly say, 'Only God is my security, the rock in whom I trust', and while we maybe do not see 'measurable results', we do sense glimpses from the one who even in the midst of disappointment and failure continues to say, 'Look I am doing a new deed, can you see it?'

---

[25] Sue Pickering, *Spiritual Direction: A Practical Introduction* (Norwich: Canterbury Press, 2008), p. 188.

Reflection

Where or when did you experience the invitation to let go of
your own efforts and struggle, and just go with the flow – the
flow of God's providence? When did you experience a
broader, more expansive horizon wherein some of your own
controls dissolved a little? Maybe you can let go a little now,
especially in some area of your life where there is struggle, and
in that letting go you may glimpse 'that which is too beautiful
to die'.

CHAPTER 14

Loosening the Grip:
Lessons in Detachment

He who binds to himself a joy
Does the winged life destroy;
But he who kisses the joy as it flies
Lives in eternity's sunrise.

'ETERNITY', WILLIAM BLAKE

The hardest of all life's lessons, I think, are those relating to detachment. This is primarily because our significant relationships, roles, even our posessions can define us to the extent that we depend on them for our sense of self and our self-image. Detachment brings freedom from this dependence, it is not about numbing out, but more about loosening the grip. Even the joys must not be gripped too tightly, or they too could 'the winged life destroy'. The disciples had a great time up the mountain, so great they wanted to stay there and set up camp: 'Lord, it is wonderful for us to be here, if you want I will make three shelters here' (Mt 17:1). Like all of us, they wanted to stay in the dazzling light and hold onto it forever. In that moment they had relief from the impending trials awaiting them, they were together and enjoying this oneness and bliss. Sometimes we have a wonderful experience in nature or on a retreat or on holidays and we want to hold onto it. Great moments like these can be mood–altering, changing our perceptions for a while and sometimes offering a new state of consciousness.

Romantic love can be in this realm, whereby we lose our own sense of separateness (and critical faculties) as we are taken up with that feeling of being besotted by the 'perfect other', and they besotted with us. At the risk of sounding cynical and negating all that the movies and advertising sell us, this dazzling light inevitably fades, and the perfect other can appear at times anything but dazzling. When we encounter the imperfect reality of the other (and that of ourselves), then the real work of relationship begins and we start to negotiate what it is to love somebody for better, for worse.

Searching for the Spark

'I'm not in love anymore, the spark is gone. I don't love him like I used to,' a lady shared with me once. She was considering her options, to leave her second marriage for the same reasons as she left her first, or to take a journey to discover what this 'spark' might really mean for her. So much around her would endorse the opinion that she should follow her need for a new, dazzling experience. Deep down, I think, she wasn't so sure. The disciples weren't so sure either after they had to come down from their dazzling experience on the mountain and face ordinary life again. Both the woman seeking the spark in relationships and the disciples seeking it through religious experience had to learn deeper lessons. When we depend on anything from the outside, any stimulus to 'keep the spark alive', inevitably we will be disappointed.

Longing for Paradise

When we were born, we enjoyed a sense of unity with our mothers, an oceanic oneness, where we were merged together. This symbiotic union meant we did not have a separate identity. Later we had to separate out, but the memory of that perfect union remains somewhere inside. The love that was external becomes internalised, so we can trust the love from within. This gives us an inside knowledge that we are lovable and unique, so we don't have to keep craving it from the outside. Depending on the level of internalisation that took place, we may continue to carry a longing to regain that sense of oneness and union. A theory developed by John Bowlby and Mary Ainsworth suggests that our attachment to our primary caregivers (usually our mothers) determines how we engage and maintain contact with others throughout our lives. Much of our abandonment or engulfment patterns can be traced back to how we bonded, or failed to bond, with our caregivers. We often transfer that longing for bonding onto potential relationships where we imagine we can regain that paradise of oneness again. The difficult learning is that it is not the *fusion* of selves, but rather our *separate* selves that create real relationship.

We will always long for relationship, we are social beings, and we are made for connection and community. It would be a pathological illness to turn away from relationship. In fact, healthy brain development, as well as a healthy immune system, depends on interpersonal contact. We long to be mirrored back to ourselves in order to know our own intrinsic worth and value. Many of us exit childhood with quite a deficit of mirroring. However, when we look for that mirroring through constant reassurance in adult life, we put a heavy burden on relationships, we trade intensity for intimacy. Scripture cautions us about this external approval seeking: 'how can you believe since you look to one another for approval and are not concerned with the approval that comes from God' (Jn 5:31-47). We sometimes look towards others to fill up the empty spaces inside ourselves, but when we do this the consequence is twofold: others may feel used, and we will feel disappointed. We might cling desperately out of this longing for bonding or alternatively we might push away due to fear of disappointment. Neither forms a good basis for relationship. Furthermore, try to imagine a relationship where one is desperately trying to cling (fear of separation) and the other is desperately pushing away (fear of engulfment).

When we consider the complexity of relationships, it might sound like good advice to tell people to run as fast as they can in the opposite direction the next time they see that special stranger looking at them across a crowded room. That kind of advice would make life very bland and colourless; after all, the complexity is part of the magic of all our relationships. However, we would save ourselves much heartache if we knew that nobody or nothing can give us what we are refusing to give ourselves. The loving look can only reflect back what we know to be already within ourselves; it cannot give us something that is not already true about us.

The marigolds outside my window look beautiful today, the sun has opened them up and brought out the beauty that is within them. Likewise, other people can bring out the truth of who we are. They can, like the sun, highlight and reflect back our beauty and goodness, but it is not their light which 'gives us' this beauty. Our hearts were created in a way that only Divine Love can complete them, but we get glimpses of that love through others. Pierre Teilhard de Chardin, the French philosopher, tells us: 'Divine Love is capable of uniting living beings in such a way as to complete and fulfil them, for it alone takes them and joins them by what is deepest in themselves.'[26]

Just Looking at Us

I am sitting at the table, writing up some notes for work – not in a particularly upbeat mood. It is one of those ordinary grey days, dishes piled up in the sink, thoughts piled up in my mind, some of them not so generous: *why doesn't he wash them just once!* There is a lot on the to-do list today – a bit like every other day. I glance up, still preoccupied with my to-do list. Pat, my husband, is looking over smiling at me. 'What?' I say in one of my cranky, defensive tones. 'Nothing,' he replies calmly, and continues to smile. 'Why are you looking at me?' I continue to ask, and then I remember my uncombed hair, and ask suspiciously again 'Why are you looking, what's wrong with me this time?' 'There's nothing wrong,' he repeats, 'I'm just looking at you.' I think that's what God is doing, on ordinary 'bad hair days'. When we are not even noticing, God is 'just looking', not finding something wrong with us, just looking at

---

[26] Pierre Teilhard de Chardin, *The Phenomenon of Man*, trans. by Bernard Wall and introduction by Julian Huxley (London: William Collins Sons and Co. Ltd, 1959), p. 291.

us, but we assume there's something wrong with us, or that something is going to be demanded of us. In that moment, Pat communicated a glimpse of God to me, no longer aware of my uncombed hair, and I saw the divine glance illuminated – a transfiguration moment. It would be lovely to pitch our tents in this harmonious moment, but tomorrow, most likely, I will reassume the cranky tone, and he will once again be the one who leaves his unwashed mug around the house, the fallible one who has that unsavoury habit of resting his muddy boots on the coffee table. But for now, for this moment, without any expectation that it stay this way, I am nourished by that reminder of how the Divine simply likes looking at us.

No human being can be the total source of unconditional love, no person can give us perfect attunement. They have their own moods, their own internal rhythms and their own differing needs for space and contact. Our longing for perfect attunement can keep us in cycles of broken relationships and reactivated disappointment, seeking one 'mood-altering' romantic love after another. We may feel anger and a sense of loss that the other is not always perfectly reliable and consistently adjusted to our narcissistic needs. Instead of embracing the transience of everything, we try to control the uncontrollable, and in so doing we become severed from our true selves, outwardly dependent and inwardly depleted – the ground of addiction.

Spaces in Togetherness
The poet Kahlil Gibran advises us to keep a space of awareness in our relationships.

> … let there be spaces in your togetherness,
> And let the winds of Heaven dance between you.
> Love one another, but make not a bond of love:
> Let it rather be a moving sea between the shores of your souls.[27]

[27] Kahlil Gibran, *The Prophet* (1923) (New York: Alfred A. Knopf, 2001), p. 9.

When we truly see ourselves and what expectations we are bringing into relationships, there is space to see the magic and wonder of the other. And then, whether we have wonderful Mount Tabor experiences or great moments of connection, we do not need to cling, but we can thank this person, this moment for the gift that they are, without placing burdens that they stay that way! We can, like Peter in the gospel, say, 'it is wonderful to be here', and let the moment go. We can even receive that 'dangerous look' across the crowded room, knowing it is but a glimpse of our ultimate source of unconditional love and fulfilment. Allowing ourselves to receive this unconditional love, we can be freed from our own enslaved dependence on others to give us our sense of worth. Much of our fearful co-dependence in relationship would subside if we knew already that we are the beloved – with all the dignity and beauty of knowing inside who we really are, 'the spirit bears witness that we are children of God (Rm 8:16). This, of course, is the journey of a lifetime, so in the meantime let us be gentle with ourselves and one another for our neediness and insecurities.

Reflection

'You are my Beloved' (Rm 1:7). Hear these words addressed to you. Receive them and know it is not because of anything you do, but simply because you are looked upon with love. Relax, and visualise God looking at you with delight. Allow divine love to gaze upon you; 'as a bridegroom rejoices over his bride, so will your God rejoice over you' (Is 62:5). Take a few moments to let these words trickle from the head to the heart. Allow the words to resonate inside your heart, especially wherever you doubt yourself and wherever there are wounds that leave you feeling unlovable. Think about the people in your own story who may have communicated a glimpse of how God sees you – can you receive the gift they are offering to you?

CHAPTER 15

To Sulk or Not to Sulk:
When Life Isn't Fair

The acceptance of oneself is the essence of the moral problem and the epitome of a whole outlook on life.[28]

CARL JUNG

A few children and their father played on the beach; they laughed and screamed as they buried each other in sand. It was a banquet of sun, rain, wind, sand, dirt, sweat, tears and laughter. Suddenly there was an angry scream. 'No, it's not fair, that's my spade he's playing with. Give me back my spade!' His dad tried to cajole him, encouraging him to allow his baby brother to have his spade for a while, but to no avail. The boy gradually removed himself from the party and sat on the rocks, head in hands, muttering, 'It's not fair, that's my spade.' The others called him back, saying, 'Come on, David, there are other spades. Look, we're having some ice cream now.' Eventually they gave up and they continued to play, laugh and eat, while David watched from a distance. At times he looked like he was going to go back over and join them, but then he retreated inside himself again and pulled his protective coat closer around him. Letting go to the fun and joining in the party would also mean letting go of his precious sulk. He continued to mutter, 'It's not fair, he took what is

---

[28] Carl Jung, *Modern Man in Search of a Soul*, p. 235.

mine.' David obviously felt like he would lose or seem weak if he gave in, or if he let go the 'terrible injustice' done to him, and so the choice to sulk or not to sulk remained. In the end, no one even noticed that he was sulking (or noticed he was missing from the group), so he just gave up and returned tentatively, although still muttering 'It's not fair'.

It's Not Fair!

The father in the story of the prodigal son had a hard job trying to convince the elder brother to let go of his sulk and join with his younger brother and the party. I think the elder brother was also probably muttering, 'It's not fair, he took what is mine.' Scripture tells us that he refused to go in. Many times we long to join in the full banquet of life but our sulk prevents us and we hold on to our position, convincing ourselves that 'it's not fair'. No, life was never, and it never will be fair. If we insist that life *should* be fair, we will be continually frustrated. I am often inspired by those people who have the most reason to declare the unfairness of life, and yet they are often the ones who seem most able to see the blessing in their story, and most willing to do something to change what has been unfair in their own lives, or in the life of another.

Anne shared with me something of her spirituality and her life. She was quietly spoken and barely audible when she talked about herself. She was small in stature, walked slowly, careful of over-exerting her muscles that had been weak since birth. She had an unassuming and gentle smile. Her mother had died when Anne was young, as had her best friend. She was a little girl alone in the world, with no one who she felt believed in her. She was left in a world that did not see her and labelled her as 'slow'. She seemed to be often left doing hard manual jobs, despite often being in pain due to wasted muscles on one side of her body. She was abused physically and emotionally, and felt unable to tell anyone as she had believed it was her own fault. She stopped attending school, so she never learned how to read and write. She carried the labels that society gave her all through her life; she believed that she had nothing to offer, which eventually led her to an attempt to take her own life. Anne's feelings of low self-worth were endorsed the day she was coming out of the effects of the overdose, and heard someone say, 'Sure if she had died, who would miss her anyway.' All I could think while listening to her story was, 'What has happened to this woman is not fair – life is not fair.' But this was not how Anne now saw it. She had chosen life against all the odds, she had looked at nature and noticed how it survived through the harsh winters, and made up her mind that she would too. She had called out to God and to her mother, as something inside her now disregarded the labels. She began to search for her life and for her truth. She dreamed of pencils and words and went back to adult education (she now helps other adults with learning difficulties). She dreamed of finding her voice, of telling someone about her childhood traumas, so she started writing a journal addressed to her mother, and began to tell her story in counselling. She grieved the pain of her lost childhood through her journals and then she read them aloud to me. I listened as she read in her quiet, unassuming voice, I listened to this amazing person whom society had labelled slow and unimportant, I listened as she told her story with such dignity, truth and courage.

Anne reminds me of the Canaanite woman in the gospel, the unnamed woman who came in from the outside, who, on feeling unheard, persevered, believing in a truth inside her, and Jesus affirmed her saying 'Woman, you have great faith' (Mt 15:28). Anne is also a woman of great faith, who persevered in finding her voice and bearing witness to a truth inside her. She reminds us that those who are 'unnamed' in our society, without a voice or labelled and pushed aside, must be given back their voice. We must listen to them as they call to us from the margins. Anne still has difficulty with making her voice heard, but she does not need to shout, because even in her whisper I believe she is prophetic. For me, she has been a spiritual teacher. She teaches me to have a more childlike but profound faith, one of total trust that cannot be accessed through study or any academic ambition. I feel grateful to God 'for hiding these things from the learned and the clever and revealing them to little children' (Lk 10:21).

Anne does not hide behind the sulk of life's unfairness; she has no time for victimisation, but has channelled her energy to come forward and is growing in confidence every day, and in finding her voice, gives permission to other unheard voices to come forward also.

Reflection

Who around you as been labelled as 'slow' or unimportant? Whose voice has been silenced or unheard? Maybe there is someone you pass by each day, but have never really heard or seen. Perhaps it may even be a part of yourself that you have never heard or seen, a part you have silenced or rejected? Spend a little time journaling about the labels that have silenced the unheard or forgotten voices around you, or within you.

CHAPTER 16

On the Road to Someone Important: Wholeness or Holiness?

If the deepest ground of my being is love, then in that very love itself and nowhere else will I find myself, and the world, and my brother in Christ.[29]

THOMAS MERTON

I f my friends in Ireland could see me now, I mused, standing on the stage of a large theatre in Perth, Western Australia. It was the opening night of a theatrical production that I had written and produced, now being staged in Australia following a tour of Ireland. It was a modern interpretation of the writings and life of Thérèse of Lisieux entitled *Shower of Roses,* and it had taken off beyond all expectation, first in Ireland and now in Australia. Armed with flowers, coming off stage, I was handed a note. It was an invitation from someone I considered an expert on spirituality, a holy person. Apparently, she had great interest in the writings of Thérèse and other mystics and wished to talk to me about the play. She lived a long journey away, and I would be collected by car.

I headed off the next day with a friend who had travelled from Ireland with me. I was excited about the prospect of meeting this woman to discuss the play that I had written, and hopefully discover more about the writings of Thérèse and talk about the music, drama and dance that were part of the production.

---

[29] Thomas Merton, *Contemplation in a World of Action* (New York: Doubleday, 1971), p. 7.

I missed the name of the driver who collected us. She chatted about the play, and what aspect of it she herself connected with. She talked about her struggle with her own faith, her husband's depression. I noticed her chipped fingernails as I half-listened, distracted by thoughts of the night before and all the affirmation I had received about the production, as well as wondering about this important person we were travelling to meet. Finally, we arrived at our destination – a rather austere-looking convent, and waited for some time in a parlour where I eventually met the woman I had so longed to meet. She was holding a copy of the script of my play, and a red pen. She asked me questions, but didn't wait for the answers. She asked such things as 'How could you know anything about the dark night of the soul?' I attempted a reply and she quickly interrupted, 'The dark night of the soul is a sublime experience reserved only for souls of great sanctity, so how could *you* know?' My hands felt clammy as I attempted to nibble on a biscuit offered by a young novice (as she genuflected). The novice was introduced to me as 'the one who forgets to turn off the 100-watt bulb in the corridor at night'. Suddenly I longed for fresh air! This woman, whom I had put on a pedestal, continued to run her red Biro over some words on the script, pausing now and then to ask me questions, such as what did I know of the mystical experiences of John of the Cross. She went on to talk about her own religious calling, and how she had to 'lay down her life' in order to live in this way. I wondered what she had to 'lay down' and thought that whatever it was, it might be better that she take it up again! Eventually, she said she had duties to perform and visitors waiting.

Seeing the Sacred in the Ordinary

As we returned to the car, I reflected on 'holiness' without wholeness. We returned to our driver, who smiled, perhaps knowingly. On the journey back I paid much more attention to her when she spoke about herself, her struggle with faith, her husband's illness, and this time I even saw her eyes, which looked tired. I hadn't noticed the 'holiness' of her smile earlier as I had been focused on meeting someone 'more important'. I even noticed the guys on the streets, whom I also had missed on the journey outwards, those with ghetto blasters and tattoos, and wondered about their dark nights and mystical experiences. Somehow, the mundane seemed charged with the sacred and I wanted to genuflect as I watched a man put out the garbage, and wondered who he was 'laying down his life for' that day.

Following that experience, I think I have learnt to project less expectation and adulation onto 'holy people', whereby I missed the holiness of everyone around me. In some way my sight was restored, in receiving an awakening of that which is already around us – the miracles, the sublime experiences, the mystical moments, and those of great sanctity. God's presence shines brighter than all the 100-watt bulbs in the world, but we could miss the experiences and the holiness of those on our path when we are only focused on reaching the end of the road – to meet 'someone important'.

Following Our Calling

We can sometimes try, with great willpower, to follow what we think is our vocation, or God's will, whereby we sometimes follow those voices that tell us *we should, we ought to, it is our duty to lay down our lives.* These demands can feel harsh and are no respecters of our sometimes frail natures, and when they come in demanding, forceful ways, they are usually more our own critical inner voices than that of the Spirit. Internal forces can tell us to take up our cross or do huge sacrificial things but, without love, can leave us joyless and frustrated. Perhaps in the past we often misunderstood the concept of 'vocation' and placed an over-emphasis on what we would do for God rather than what God would do in and through us. We all know people who have carried their cross pretty well but have never learnt how to carry the Love of God so well. I have often heard the expression 'hardening of the oughteries', which is indeed something very real, because the 'oughts' and the 'shoulds' can leave very hardened hearts. When our good works or service is done because we 'ought to' (while we remain severed from our hearts), others will not be moved, no matter how charitable we are towards them (they may not even have wished to be helped in the first place). Sometimes the greatest service and greatest vocation we can offer is to simply share with another the gift of who we are, our very being, including our weaknesses. When God visits our lives, it is not with a list of should or oughts, but rather through an experience – a fire burning in our hearts, a spring welling up inside, or a cup running over. When we trace those moments of fire, or springs, we will discern something of how the Spirit is drawing us. There is usually a pattern about how this call is issued to us, and it is congruent with our deepest dream and our deepest gifts. Frederick Buechner, American writer and theologian, tells us vocation is 'where our greatest passion meets the world's greatest need'.[30] Likewise, Parker Palmer says, 'Before I can tell my life what I want to do with it, I must listen to my life telling me who I am.'[31] It is as if our life's purpose is deeply built into us, almost inside our DNA, so our most important task is to listen attentively from within.

Reflection

Remember the times when there was a fire burning in your heart – times you felt alive, a sense of purpose, where you felt aligned to a flow of life within. Remember a time when you knew you were making a valuable contribution and your gifts were being manifested in a way that brought joy to yourself and others. What do you notice about those times, what characteristics had these experiences? How do they differ from the times you followed a list of shoulds and oughts that may have hardened your heart, engendering tension around you? What have been the times of your deepest gladness, and how

---

[30] Quoted in *The Reflective Counselor: Daily Meditations for Lawyers*, F. Gregory Coffey, Maureen C. Kessler (Chicago: American Bar Association, 2008), p. 119.
[31] Parker Palmer, *Let Your Life Speak: Listening for the Voice of Vocation* (San Francisco: Jossey-Bass, 2000), p. 2.

did they meet the world's deepest sadness? Ask the Spirit to help you discern how you might be called to 'lay down your life' and leave behind something so that you are free to 'fan into flame the gift that God gave you' (2 Tm 1:7).

CHAPTER 17

The Right Mark on the Door: Unanswered Prayers

Not 'til the loom is silent and the shuttles cease to fly,
Shall God unroll the canvas
And explain the reason why.
The dark threads are as needful in the Weaver's skilful
*   hand,*
As the threads of gold and silver
In the pattern He has planned.

'THE WEAVER', BENJAMIN FRANKLIN

It was the morning of my wedding. All through the night I kept the candle lit, hoping there might be a miracle by morning: maybe my mother would arrive dressed up in her mother of the bride outfit, which she had chosen. Maybe she would be able to share the delight of seeing the lovely wedding dress and shawl she had carefully stitched for me. Maybe, maybe. Still hopeful, I rang the hospital and asked to be put through to her. I heard a faint 'Hello', then the sound of her getting sick. 'Hello, Mam, this is Mart,' I said. To my dismay I heard a faltering voice say, 'Who, who is it?' My voice broke and I tried to reply, 'Mam, it's the morning of my wedding.' No reply. The nurse came on the line then and said, 'She's very tired.' There would be no miracle. The nightmare had really happened; that horrific accident did really happen two weeks earlier, when my mother was putting final touches to the wedding clothes. Now she was lying in a hospital bed and missing the day she had looked forward to so much. She was the one who was to give me away – she talked of little else in the weeks before that awful moment. Now here at the ceremony I could think of little else except that awful accident and my mother lying in the hospital bed, my heart breaking at her absence.

Where is God in This?

'Where is God in this?' someone asked as they looked at Mam's body racked in pain on what should have been one of the happiest days of her life. The nurses seemed to be silently asking that too as they looked on from a distance, eyes filled with tears, when we visited Mam after the ceremony. Some people didn't want to see, didn't want to hear. 'She'll be fine again,' they said, trying to console me, or perhaps it was themselves they were consoling. But she would not be fine again, there was no dressing this up. One day as I watched my mother being hoisted from her bed onto a stretcher, her broken body wrenched in pain, perspiration flowing down her vulnerable face, I angrily asked God, 'Where are you now?' I seemed to hear an unexpected and prompt reply: 'I am there, being hoisted onto the stretcher, perspiration flowing down my vulnerable face.' That was not the answer I wanted to hear. I needed a more powerful God who would fight this terrible tragedy and, above all, do something! I did not want this God of helplessness, vulnerability. I did not want a God of tears and perspiration. I missed him that day and over the following weeks until Mam's death in the hours between Christmas night and St Stephen's morning. There was no happy ending, no meaningful goodbyes; no philosophical reasons as to the 'why' of it all, no silver lining – just raw pain and unanswered questions.

The weeks and months that followed were filled with clichés, my own and those of others: *It was a happy day for her; she's in a better place now; you wouldn't want for her to suffer anymore.* The final straw was when someone said, 'Maybe she was not meant to give you away at the wedding because that's a man's job.' That was it, no more clichés or platitudes. I closed off the questions (and closed off my sorrow), nursing a cynical attitude towards this 'all-powerful God'.

Sharing the Suffering

Many months later I sat with a wise and humble woman, a spiritual director, who asked me about my mother's death. I told her the story of how let down I felt by God, how angry I felt that he didn't protect my mother that awful morning of the accident. I spilled out the hopes, the dreams we shared and how they had all been shattered. I grieved both the loss of my mother and the loss of the all-powerful God I had once trusted. I lamented how I used to believe that if we prayed, God would protect us from tragedy, from 'the worst imaginable things happening to us'. She listened, her eyes filled with compassion. There were no clichés, no solutions offered. I felt my pain was really heard. Her eyes communicated a sad and palpable empathy. I felt she was just feeling the pain with me, and somehow in her silence I began to feel as if it was no longer her but Christ there, suffering with me. The all-powerful God was dismantled; now there stood a silent, suffering Christ holding out a nail-scarred hand. Somehow I started to intuit that he too knew what awful suffering was, he knew what it was like to have 'the worst imaginable thing happen'. The sadness was not taken, but some of the anger was, and in the silence something softened. There were still no answers, and though I knew I would never get my wedding day back or ever get my mother back, I sensed I was beginning to get myself back.

Sometimes our prayers can have an Old Testament ring to them. We believe if we pray hard enough, we will, like the chosen people, be spared of bad things happening. We think, if we are amongst those with 'the right mark on the door', the angel of death will pass us by. Did Jesus himself have the right mark on his door? Did the angel of death pass him by when he faced the most unimaginable death? When Jesus asked Peter, and asks us also, 'Who do you say I am? (Mk 8:27), will our response be big enough to hold the suffering and unfairness of life, or is our God a cosy, magical one? Do we believe that when good things happen, we think it is because we are special, singled out for special privileges? And consequently, when bad things happen, do we think we are out of favour with God? When the prophet Job went through his series of disasters, people wondered what he may have done wrong, why he had not the right mark on the door, and presumed he must be a false prophet. He got clichés preached at him too – and he more or less told them, 'I could speak as you do if I was in your place.' He asked, 'Will no one teach you to be quiet – the only wisdom that becomes you' (Job 13:5). We can try to use our prayers as insurance against suffering in an attempt to ensure that the awful things won't happen to us. Scripture does not tell us that we will be spared suffering if we live a spiritual life, but it does say that a presence would be with us always throughout our lives. 'And look, I am with you always, yes, to the end of time' (Mt 28:20).

Reflection

Remember a time of suffering in your life, a time when 'the worst imaginable' happened for you. What prayers did you think were not answered? How did you feel towards God? What happened to you, in your faith, following that time, and what changed in your image of God, in your image of yourself? Who is God for you now? When Jesus asks, 'Who do you say I am', what do you say?

CHAPTER 18

Joy and Sorrow Unmasked:
Allowing Our Tears

Your joy is your sorrow unmasked.
And the selfsame well from which your
laughter rises was oftentime filled with your tears.[32]

KAHLIL GIBRAN

We live in continuous cycles of births and deaths, and the measure to which we feel our grief is the measure to which we feel our joy. Choosing to acknowledge and live our losses fully disposes us to engage in life with more openness and with less need for guaranteed outcomes. 'We believe that the investment of our love is worth it, for we have entered into the mystery of life where the hellos that follow our goodbyes are our guideposts to the eternal home.'[33]

We experience grief when we lose any person or thing with whom we have an attachment that defines us in some way; or one that offers security, safety, comfort, status. These losses may include not just relationships with persons, but with pets, places, stages of life. We may also grieve the loss of a career or job; we may discover that we feel a loss of identity. We cannot say one type of loss is inherently more difficult than another, as it is the investment of ourselves and the attachment involved that creates the degree of loss we are experiencing.

---

[32] Khalil Gibran, *The Prophet*, p. 29.
[33] Joyce Rupp, *Praying Our Goodbyes* (Notre Dame: Ave Maria Press, 1988), p. 26.

'Goodbyes are any of those times when we find ourselves without someone or something that has given our life meaning and value, when a dimension of our life seems to be out of place or unfulfilled.'[34]

Obstacles to Grief

We can sometimes defend ourselves against our grief. Our culture often carries subtle, and not so subtle, messages to prevent us expressing our grief. We interject many myths that suggest our pain will go away if we ignore it, overcome or push beyond it. We are offered ways to go out and purchase something or to employ positive attitudes to cajole ourselves out of our grief. When a loved one dies, we are told that the grieving process lasts a year, and after that we are somehow over the loss. There is also a suggestion in our society that we need to be 'strong' in the face of grief, and it could be interpreted that this disposition of strength involves not falling to pieces or expressing too many tears. These myths, if taken on board, can result in us feeling abnormal if we don't adhere to them, or it might mean some well-intentioned friends do not bring up the deceased person's name in case it upsets us. Of all these myths or clichés, the most difficult are the 'spiritual' ones where we are told 'it is God's will', 'they're better off now'.

Stages of Grief

In a culture that no longer holds many external rituals of grief, such as the customs of wearing black and abstaining from social events, we need to be creative about honouring the stages of our grief. It can be difficult to honour the grieving process when there is complicated grief, such as when there is unfinished business, sudden death, a relationship where the person had treated us badly or we have regrets around our relationship with them. Our beliefs and attitudes about death, the depth of the relationship and circumstances surrounding

---

[34] Ibid.

the death all affect how we go through the grieving process. However, it is generally understood that we go through certain stages in our losses, generally: shock, denial, anger, bargaining, depression and acceptance. It is helpful to know about these stages when we are grieving or when we are accompanying another in grief, but it would be untrue to say that we go through the stages in any chronological order or within certain timeframes. It would be quite usual to go back and forth, to get stuck in one stage for a while or to bypass another. Sometimes we think we are out of the difficult feelings when we enter a bargaining stage, but it is not the same as the final stage of acceptance. 'It looks like peace, but it is not peace yet; it is a truce.'[35] This truce is a desperate attempt to protect ourselves from the dark phase of nothingness or depression. It is our way of clutching at straws where one 'asks and hopes for a little extension, usually to finish unfinished business.'[36] Just when we think we have completed the process, we hear a song or conversation or the person's name, and we are right back in the middle of the grief again and may wonder, 'Will I ever get over it?'

Accompanying Others in Grief

However eloquent our theology and our words, they cannot compare to a pastoral heart – one that thumps with real compassion. When we truly enter into the dilemma of another person (like the spiritual guide did for me around the death of my mother), and meet them as a guest in their inner world, we enter into a sacramental moment. Simple gestures can be sacramental – a look, a smile, a touch – when they communicate presence.

We need to have awareness of our own patterns of grieving and awareness of our avoidances if we are to accompany another safely in this difficult journey. We also need to be aware

---

[35] Elisabeth Kübler-Ross, *Living with Death and Dying* (London: Souvenir Press, 1982), p. 38.
[36] Ibid., p. 39.

of various traditions, customs and approaches to loss and grief so as not to have just one way of seeing or dealing with loss. Above all, we need to be able to provide an empathic, non-judgemental space for someone to explore their grief in – whatever stage they find themselves at. We need to meet each other as God does – right in the middle of our denial, or whatever protective mechanisms we employ. Sometimes denial is an appropriate stage whereby 'we need escape as a necessary part of the grieving process. When we are bereaved, we feel our loss has been too inconsolable to accept.'[37]

In accompanying someone who is grieving, the 'less is more' approach is very powerful, along with a respectful use of silence. This can help to bring us out of 'heady' places of denial and into the truth of how we are in our feelings and in our bodies. This is especially important as we tend to disconnect from our bodies and from the present moment when we are splitting from our grief. Paradoxically, through the silence, and sometimes by abstaining from the offering of 'consoling words', we help someone to feel their experience of grief and come into compassionate relationship with it, which is the true path to healing. It is important that we do not intrude with too many words or questions. The person needs to tell the story and grieve for herself/himself as well as the person or thing that has been lost (we grieve mostly for ourselves).

Spiritual Crisis
When somebody is grieving a loss of a sense of God, or loss of a comforting God image, it is generally referred to as a spiritual crisis, and this can be very painful. It is tempting to rush in with consoling God images. This, however, may be an obstacle to the bereaved person. When all those images that served as scaffolding have crumbled and fallen, much anger can be directed towards God. The grief and anger here are very real,

---

[37] Mildred Tengbom, *Grief for a Season* (Minnesota: Bethany House Publishers, 1989), p. 34.

as is the sense of abandonment, but the constant, steady presence of one who listens can provide a safe space while deaths and births take place in the soul. 'Both birth and death are times of transition for the soul, times when we particularly need loving guides and witnesses.'[38]

Eventually, new landscapes emerge in the person's journey, but they come from within the person's own process and usually not from any good advice offered. We are prepared for the final passing from this world by living through the death of others, and in not denying them, we learn to embrace their beauty and pain as part of the mystery of our lives. We come to accept that every embrace has a goodbye somewhere in it, every togetherness a loneliness and every beautiful memory a tinge of sadness; 'there will always be a corner of our hearts where it is autumn, that part of us which aches with searching and loneliness, with restlessness or dissatisfaction.'[39] Paradoxically, it is when we name and experience these autumnal spaces, we will be able to embrace the first signs of spring in the healing process of grief and loss.

Reflection

Where in your heart is the season of autumn? What ache, loss or loneliness needs to be honoured? Who or what are you missing? Can you make space for this autumn season even where there is togetherness or joy? Allow a few quiet moments to hold the joy and sorrow together in the 'selfsame well'.

---

[38] Elisabeth Kübler-Ross, *Living with Death and Dying*, p. 75.
[39] Joyce Rupp, *Praying Our Goodbyes*, p. 24.

CHAPTER 19

Feet Washing:
Looking Out for One Another

If I, then, the Lord and Master have washed your feet, you must wash each other's feet.

JOHN 13:14

'Try to look out for each other' was one of the last things my mother said when she felt she was coming near the end of her life. It is when we feel we are nearing the end that we often say the important things; rarely do we hear someone say, 'I wish I had kept the kitchen tidier'. We usually hear something about relationships, something we want to leave behind. Jesus said something similar: 'Love one another as I have loved you.' He told his followers that he himself had to leave the world, but he would leave an inner guide for each one of us – the indwelling Holy Spirit. He promised we would never be alone, and that each time we looked out for each other, we would be continuing his mission on earth. This 'looking out for one another' embodies the presence of Christ in the world. Sometimes, it is not even necessary that we are present physically; we can look out for one another in our thoughts. I think we are all connected by invisible vibrational chords, so we can send blessings, well-intentioned thoughts, even healing along these chords. We might feel a subtle nudge to ring somebody, send a card or say a prayer. So many times we just keep with the timetable of our day and ignore these subtle 'interruptions'.

It was about two weeks after Christmas. My phone beeped, I recognised the number, and it was somebody that I had not met in about two years. I answered the call but all I heard was a lot of voices, and the clattering of plates. Perhaps, I said to myself, she was in a restaurant and she pressed my number by mistake, or maybe the phone was in the bottom of her bag. I decided to ignore it, but then wondered, will I ring her back? No, that would be silly, if she needs me she can ring again. She did not ring back, but about two months later I received a phone call from her, asking if we could meet. After she had apologised for not making contact in about two years, she went on to tell me about a terrible crisis she had gone through when she had no one to advise her on a course of action at the time. She had terminated a pregnancy, which she now said was not the right decision for her. 'Did you talk to anybody? I asked. 'No,' she said, 'I thought of ringing you, but just didn't have the courage to pick up the phone.' I asked her when this crisis happened. 'Oh, about two weeks after Christmas,' she replied.

Later that evening I felt very sad as I reflected back on what had happened; she had nobody to help her in her panic, her phone had 'accidentally' rang through to mine, but unfortunately I had dismissed my deeper intuition and followed that voice that said *don't be silly*. Maybe today someone wants to ring you but just can't pick up the phone; maybe somebody needs you to send them thoughts of healing or a blessing today. Listen carefully – if you feel drawn to contact somebody, even if something in you says *don't be silly*, do it anyway; when there is something happening on that connecting line between you and somebody else, listen to your intuition, it may be telling you to 'pick up' your receiver.

Connecting from the Heart

Real healing cannot happen when we are helping someone out of a sense of superiority, or from using learnt skills or techniques. I remember many years ago doing a course on pastoral counselling where we learnt the skill of listening, a type of reflecting back and repeating what the client says. This is fine for a first stage, but if it continues as a technique without any real compassion from the heart, it will not connect.

In the weeks coming up to my mother's death, a man from a caring profession used to visit her. He often asked her how she was, he reflected back her answers with great precision – he repeated exactly what he had heard, and he made all the correct interventions and responses. He shook hands with her respectfully and made the appropriate eye contact. My mother was a gracious woman who rarely said anything offensive. One day she called me aside and said, 'Do you know that nice man who visits me and asks me the questions? Would you please ask him politely not to come back anymore.'

While he was indeed a nice man and good in intention, there was heart missing in the conversations. She went on to request that I would call the doctor, 'the one who knows what I need'. I beckoned to each doctor that passed, asking my mother if he or she was the one she was looking for. She shook her head to each one of them, but finally she said, 'That's her, that's the doctor who knows me best.' She waved over to the petite young girl who worked as a nurse's aide. 'Ah there you are,' said my mother to the young girl, who quietly plumped up my mother's pillows, 'you know me best.' This young girl was indeed a doctor, a doctor of the heart – and because she 'knew her best', there was healing in each encounter between her and my mother.

When people met Jesus, they met a heart thumping with compassion. They met somebody capable of entering into their pain and their dilemma. Jesus wept over the death of his friend Lazarus. There were tears, touch, spittle and earth in his healing. He did not keep a safe distance. He emptied himself, 'who being in the form of God did not count his equality with God something to be grasped' (Phil 2:5-8). There was a cost involved in touching the leper and reaching across ethnic and religious boundaries. He did not elevate himself in his ministry, in fact it was the faith of the other he affirmed: 'He touched their eyes and said according to your faith, let it be done' (Mt 9:29). We are reminded that we now have the privilege and responsibility of carrying on this ministry, of being like Christ in our way of seeing. 'I am not in the world but you are in the world' (Jn 17:11).

When we empty ourselves of the dictates of our ego, we are disposed to 'take off our shoes' and enter into the world of the other. The greatest treasures we often bring are, not our knowledge or our qualifications, but our own brokenness and vulnerability, because what is personal is also universal. Rarely does healing happen because of our clever words, but more often because of our compassion, our look of concern or our understanding silence. It is often when we are weak that we are strong. When we face life's great unfixables (death, suffering), we can offer something through our hearts, our eyes, our touch – not a promise that we can fix the pain, but a commitment to simply stay with, sit with, wait with.

Allowing Our Feet to be Washed

It can be more difficult to receive than to give – easier to wash the feet of others than to allow our own feet to be washed. It was Holy Thursday. The gospel was being dramatised, and someone was nominated to wash our feet. When the man nominated came round, with the basin of water and towel, I felt resistant. I didn't place my feet on the ground – I hoped he would pass me by. Personally, I prefer to wash my own feet. Peter said something similar to Jesus: 'Never; you will never wash my feet.' Peter did not understand. Likewise, I did not understand. I did, however, notice (even while my toes squirmed uncomfortably) the genuine care and sincerity with which my feet were washed. It is difficult not to be in control, difficult to admit our powerlessness and dependence. It is easier to hide behind our good works, to continually wash others' feet and never depend on anyone to wash our own. Jesus replied to Peter, 'Later you will understand' (Jn 13:7). Peter did understand, and I suppose later I understood too – I married the feet-washer!

Perhaps it is when we eventually let go of over-emphasis on hierarchy, structures and positions of superiority, in our world and in our church, and gather in little groups to 'wash each others' feet', we will be free. Only then will we be truly following the One who said, 'As I have done for you, you must do for one another' (Jn 13:14). Jesus removed his outer garment and washed Peter's feet; something beautiful would happen in our world if we removed our outer garments of pomp and power and knelt at one another's feet and allowed each other to be real, to be vulnerable, to be broken and blessed, to be like 'Eucharist' to one another.

Reflection

Imagine you are sitting in the room where the disciples are having their feet washed. Jesus eventually approaches you – he is about to wash your feet. What surfaces in your heart? What protests might emerge? What do you fear in allowing yourself to be dependent, vulnerable, not in control? Perhaps you are tired of always feet-washing, caring for others – now someone wants to care for you. Can you allow yourself to be seen, to be met, to be cared for – even if now 'you do not understand'? When the analytical mind does not understand what is happening, it creates resistance. Just acknowledge this resistance, allowing yourself to breathe and let go – breath by breath, emptying yourself of control, allowing yourself to be ministered to.

CHAPTER 20

Waiting Spaces:
A Time to Dream

*We make a god of efficiency, an idol of success, a deity
of achievement. These are the false gods that tell us we
should be gods ourselves, in charge of our lives.*[40]

GERALD G. MAY

'A h, this is too slow!' I exclaimed, turning up the
oven for the pizza to cook. It will be ready in half
the time if I raise the heat. It certainly was done in
half the time – it emerged black and burnt from the oven,
ready for the bin. Waiting does not come easy to me. I am one
of those people who presses the button on pedestrian lights,
expecting the red man to change instantly to green because
I've told him to. But life is slowly teaching me about the
wisdom of waiting, and of course I can hardly wait to learn it.

Times of waiting and transition are creative and can be full
of possibility. When we talk about transition in our lives, we
often think of decision-making, moving from A to B, and
forget the value of the waiting time in the 'in-between' space
– that rich, creative, fertile time where we rest and wait. There
is a three-phase process in transition – the ending/letting go,
the waiting space, and the new beginnings. It can be difficult
to hold the tension of the in-between space, so we often jump
from the letting-go stage to the stage of new beginnings, thus

---

[40] Gerald G. May, *The Awakened Heart: Living Beyond Addiction* (New York:
HarperCollins, 1991), p. 10.

bypassing that space of non-activity where there often lies the most creative possibility. Perhaps our fear of the unknown makes it difficult for us to embrace these waiting spaces, and so we minimise anxiety by quickly filling in the gaps (with new plans, agendas and the like). I also believe our culture does not support our living in the waiting places, and it puts high value on us knowing where we are going next, being in control, and of course always having a plan B ready! 'Thus we make a God of efficiency, an idol of success, a deity of achievement. These are the false Gods that tell us we should be Gods ourselves in charge of our lives.'[41]

Of course, there can be a type of waiting that is simply an excuse not to have to take the next step or a way of resisting taking charge of our lives. When we postpone our happiness by waiting for someone else to change or when we expect circumstances to change in order for us to be happy, then our waiting is one of avoidance. If you are stuck in this kind of passive inertia, ask yourself, what am I waiting for? Who or what am I expecting to change? Could I change my belief system? Could I take one step to activate my own evolutionary process?

However, there is another kind of waiting, one that respects the rhythms and seasons in our lives and in our hearts. The most precious things in life have to be waited for, and their processes respected and not manipulated. Nature waits in winter after her letting go in autumn. When the seed lays dormant underground, she is preparing for new life. When nature is ready, it produces again, but only after a silent, dark, hidden time under the cover of the earth. This time of waiting cannot be bypassed to artificially speed up the arrival of the spring season.

In the Fullness of Time

No matter how many times we jump up and down and beg the rose to open, she will not do it until she is in the fullness

---

[41] Ibid.

of time and not until her life force is ready. Interestingly, the Creator of the universe chose a slow waiting process – nine months hidden in the womb – to break through into our world. Through the process of the incarnation, God entered a very fragile waiting phase, in the womb of a young girl, where anything could have happened, or gone wrong, and there didn't seem to have been any plan B. The Divine grows slowly, and through hidden, silent waiting places, so we also need to have silent waiting places in times of decision and transition. When something of the old has gone, and the new is not yet visible, it is then we often feel most alive (even while feeling terrified). Sometimes being close to nature, walking by the sea or deliberately choosing places of wilderness brings us into this vast boundless place where controls are suspended for a while, and we taste the deeper longings of the soul. 'Recognising the insanity of our need to control, the desire for freedom lurches and stumbles to life within us like a newborn colt trying out its brand new legs.'[42] Flutters of excitement and moments of terror can all occur during times of transition when images of life, the self and God are now shifting; yet a deeper intimacy and trust can be born in this apparent nothingness. The vulnerability, loss of certainty, and loss of identity can thrust us into places where we feel nothing is happening and we cannot find direction. 'One may have to renounce the satisfaction of seeing growth at the time of growth.'[43]

We sometimes jump from the first phase to the third, our minds searching desperately for a way to bypass the empty waiting place. Sometimes, we look for some spiritual bandage to aid us, self-help books and courses promising us we can change our lives in ten days. They give temporary relief as we start to imagine that we can jump into this new beginning straight away without going through any empty waiting time. Jesus faced something like this in the waiting time in the

---

[42] Jane Rubietta, *Resting Place: A Personal Guide to Spiritual Retreats* (USA: Intervarsity Press, 2005), p. 128.
[43] Iain Matthew, *The Impact of God: Soundings from St John of the Cross* (London: Hodder and Stoughton, 1995), p. 60.

desert. He too was offered some quick fixes to alleviate his hunger, his powerlessness.

So rather than feverishly rushing into new action in an attempt to fill empty spaces, it would do us good to stop, to wait, to listen, to allow the new thing to emerge in its own time. Maybe this is not the time for action; maybe it is the time to replenish, to go within. Watch nature closely and allow her to teach you one of the greatest of life's lesson – the ability to wait. When we wait with a calm trust, something may emerge creatively, often in a way that surprises us, and we will hear again that trustworthy voice that seems to ask us why we doubted and worried: 'no need to recall the past, look I am doing something new, now it emerges, can you see it?' (Is 43:18).

The Spirit Hovers Over Chaos

When we wait in the autumn places of the heart and enter into a deeper listening, a shift can happen, we let go of our fearful clinging to the old, and eventually hear ourselves begin to say in surrender, *not my will but yours*. This type of contemplative waiting trusts that the Divine can visit us at any time, and we can experience an epiphany in places of chaos and wilderness. When the Spirit hovers over our chaos, she can bring forth something beautiful, whereby we are called to a new path of possibility. But we miss out on this if, in trying to control the outcome, we jump to the new beginnings, bypassing the waiting phase. We have to nourish this contemplative waiting so that during times of transition we are disposed to listen and wait. 'We must gather our fragmented selves from our distracted, exhausted, noise-polluted, and frenzied existence, so that when we say "I" there is actually a unified human person present to support that pronoun.'[44]

---

[44] Kathleen Deignan, *Thomas Merton: A Book of Hours* (Notre Dame: Sorin Books, 2007), p. 25.

Journaling Through our Waiting Times

Keeping a journal is one way to creatively intuit where the spirit may be leading you in times of change. It becomes a safe space to dream. You do not have to concern yourself with correct spelling or grammar, you can simply allow a stream of consciousness to emerge, and over time will begin to notice patterns in your life – your personal story of grace and struggle. You can, through the regular discipline of keeping a journal, discern movements of consolation and desolation, and notice the difference between times when you are grounded in the core of your being, and times of feeling ungrounded and fragmented. We each have unique personalities and so God's revelation is also unique to each of us. Through writing and noticing, our awareness deepens and we discover this subtle and individual way God communicates with us.

The journal can hold the story of our walk with God through all the landscapes of our lives, through the valleys and hilltops. We can speak and listen in our writing; we can hear the longings of our hearts and the still, small whisper of our soul's voice. It is easy to forget the amazing mystery and uniqueness of our personal story, so we need to reflect and savour those moments where we sensed the wonder and mystery of our being. We so often, like the Israelites in the Old Testament, forget how God has touched us. In such times of forgetting, we feel abandoned by God and put our trust in 'other gods', and in so doing make rash, ungrounded decisions. Keeping a journal helps us remember the times when we felt fully alive, and we can draw strength from those memories when we find ourselves going through times of waiting, dryness or darkness. Just stay true to the practice and 'show up' on the page whether you feel like it or not. Our times of seeming nothingness are as valuable as the times of great inspiration in discerning our choices or values in the spiritual life.

Reflection

Find a quiet place, a page and pen, take some time to relax, do not control what you are going to write, just be open. You might like to start by doodling; maybe you might think of a line of scripture, a line of poetry, an image, or maybe, quite simply, you might compose a letter to God (or even to yourself). Anything can be the catalyst for commencing a dialogue in this search for God – who is already searching for you. Like meditation or any spiritual practice, try not to have an agenda; just relax, trust the process and see what emerges on the page: an image, a question, a worry, whatever is present. Commit this time to listening as you write, allow it to be a form of prayer, a meditation on the page.

CHAPTER 21

What Do You Want?: Reclaiming Desire

The moment we choose, providence comes to meet us, the moment I take a stand, at that very moment providence moves us too. All sorts of things occur to help me that would not otherwise have ocurred.[45]

W. H. MURRAY

Eastern spirituality sometimes suggests that having attachment to our desires is at the root of our suffering, and that if we could let go of all the clinging to those desires, we would be free. There is great wisdom in this. However, our desires can also lead us to freedom, and much of the writings of the mystics, as well as that of Ignatian spirituality, have an emphasis on discerning what we desire. Real discernment involves knowing, or at least searching to know, what our heart truly longs for, beneath all the surface likes and dislikes. We can all identify with the woman of Samaria in her encounter with Jesus at the well. She did a fair bit of ducking and diving in avoiding the big questions and in coming to the real desire of her heart – her thirst for living water. Despite having five husbands, the deepest desire of her heart remained unmet. Through the encounter with Jesus, she discovered that she had been thirsting for God, and likewise that God was thirsting for her. She discovered what she had been truly longing for all of her life, and she saw herself truthfully for the

---

[45] Adapted from W. H. Murray, *The Scottish Himalayan Expedition* (London: J. M. Dent & Sons Ltd, 1951).

first time: 'He told me everything I ever did' (Jn 4:39). She was offered a 'spring welling up inside', something that would endure, so that she would no longer have to keep returning to this well that inevitably left her thirsty again. Jesus wished to bring her to her heart, but he did not tell her exactly what she was searching for. He allowed her to come to a realisation of it herself – she needed to name something: 'I have no husband.' It was out of this naming of her emptiness that the desire of her heart was able to be met. Consequently, the woman left her water jar and she ran to tell the village.

Many other gospel stories have a similar theme to them – an inner awakening, one that touched the heart, the whole person. And because of that experience something was left behind: a habit, an attitude, an attachment, something that was no longer needed. Likewise, when Divine Love touches us, it calls us to an awakening – to the invitation to see anew. There will inevitably be something left behind, a previous way of being, or a previous way of seeing. There may also be a moment where we are asked to make a decision between two paths, often one that is good and one that is 'apparently good'. Jesus asked Bartameus, 'What do you want?' Jesus probably knew already what this man needed, but he invited him to name his desire aloud. Bartameus replied, 'Master I want to see again' (Mt 29:34). The need for discernment often follows those moments when we have been touched by God. This touch from God is never for ourselves alone; there is always a going out to share what has been entrusted to us. Though the emotional impact may eventually fade, the memory of the moments where God has touched us lives on in our hearts. They can become cornerstones in our lives. The response to this awakening might mean we have to say a concrete 'yes' in our lives, and consequently we must say 'no' also. Only in the naming of the yes and no, do we claim what is real and true for us – otherwise we stay trapped in hesitancy. As scripture advises, 'Let your yes be yes and your no be no' (Mt 5:37).

Every 'Yes' Creates a 'No'

The moment we choose, providence comes to meet us, the moment I take a stand, at that very moment providence moves in too. All sorts of things occur to help me that would not otherwise have occurred. A whole stream of miracles issue from my stand, raising in my favour, numerous unforeseen incidents and meetings and material assistance which no one could have dreamed would ever come my way.[46]

If you are sitting in a restaurant and the waiter comes to your table to take your order, and you cannot make up your mind about what you want, he will most likely go away and will not come back until you are ready. If, however, you say 'I want chicken with veg and chips', he will write down your order and everything is put in motion to serve you – the table is laid, the chef starts to prepare the food and so on. Your decisiveness sets all this in motion, but it does not happen until you name what you want. Likewise, our desires cannot be manifested until we come to our hearts and name what these desires are. When we have said yes to something, of course this means we also live the consequences and implications of our no. I have a very annoying habit of wanting a couple of things on the menu and then if I chose one, I often regret not having chosen what someone else has chosen, and then asking to change my order. When we refuse to name our yes and our no, we trade safety for the desires of the heart, our lives become predictable and safe, but without passion or colour. 'He who loves his life loses it' (Jn 12:25-26). When we refuse to take risks, we can live safely – but exhaustingly. It can be difficult to admit that we are in fact always making choices; we actually can make choices not to make choices, simply drifting in directionless ways (which is also a choice). We then often resent those who have made decisions and presume they 'just have such good luck'!

---

[46] Ibid.

It was the night before my graduation ceremony. I was getting ready to travel to the college for the graduation when someone rang wishing me the best, and then added, 'You lucky thing, a graduation ceremony, nice things like that never happen to me.' I bit my lip to prevent me from saying that it was the culmination of many years of study, numerous assignments and endless long hours. 'Luck' is often more about making decisions and following through on them, than something landing in our laps.

It can be a moment of grace when we realise that we have, in fact, made choices to remain stuck, which may have some pay-off for us, but it is important that we not get caught up in self-blame, which makes it even more difficult to move forward. When, however, we take even one step towards the light, we give other people permission to do likewise and there is a ripple effect. Mystic and saint Catherine of Sienna advises that if you become the person you are really meant to be, you will set the whole world on fire.

The Fire Burning in Our Hearts

It doesn't interest me who you know or how you came to be here. I want to know if you will stand in the centre of the fire with me and not shrink back. It doesn't interest me where or what or with whom you have studied. I want to know what sustains you, from the inside, when all else falls away.[47]

Our energy is unavailable to us when we disconnect with the fire burning in the belly, the dormant dream within us, that innate longing to make a difference. Deep down we all want to believe we have had some impact on the world around us, and have left some trail after us when we have left this planet. Furthermore, we have been told that all this amazing potential and strength has been given to us and is dwelling within. Christ

---

[47] Oriah Mountain, 'Dreamer', *The Invitation* (London: Element, HarperCollins Publishers, 2003), p. 2.

tells us we can do the wonderful things he did on earth: 'You will do even greater things than I did because I am going to the father' (Jn 14:12). We all have an unquenchable longing for meaning, for purpose, connection, beauty, transcendence and love. The things that prevent us living from those places are usually fear of what others might think. Unfortunately, if we do not name our dream and our desires, the advertising world will move in and name them for us. It will tell us we need Botox to meet our longing for beauty, it will tell us we need a new mobile phone to meet our need for connection, and some other stimulant to give us the fire burning in our hearts.

Vision Statements

Write the vision down; inscribe it on tablets to be easily read. For the vision is for its appointed time, it hastens towards its end and it will not lie; although it may take some time, wait for it, for come it certainly will before too long. (Habakkuk 2:2)

Viktor Frankl, survivor of the Nazi concentration camps, discovered that there were certain characteristics pertaining to those who managed to survive: they had an ability to see beyond present restrictions, a sense of clear vision, a belief in that vision, and a commitment to following it through. It can be very empowering to visualise what is not yet manifested in your life, to make a choice around how you really want your life to be. Sometimes we get little glimpses – they are like soul maps that we have to interpret and work with. These glimpses have in them hints of our deepest desire, but we have to tune in, listen carefully and discern what these desires might be directing us towards. We need to begin to see a vision for ourselves, clearly in our mind's eye and with all our senses. We need to put faith and trust in this vision (without attaching fixed outcomes to it). Then follows the real work, which involves daily actions, taking risks and making choices towards fulfilling our dreams. Alongside our own effort we must also allow it to unfold naturally, allow providence to work out the responses to your desires in the most life-giving way, and then simply pay attention to any chance encounters, inner and outer promptings, and the like. The Buddhists remind us to sit lightly with our attachments and to relinquish any grasping of our desires. When we have done what we can, we need to relax and trust the process (and resist any checking on it incessantly to see what is happening)

A clear belief system or mission statement and ability to visualise are the hallmarks of organisational success. Hesitancy is dangerous to our inner zest. The Israelites hesitated, drew back at their entrance to the Promised Land. We too let inner fears and doubts draw us back and so we often live without a compass, without any fire in the belly. Jesus knew what a clear mission statement was. He knew that he came to fulfil something entrusted to him: 'My food is to do the will of my father' (Jn 4:34). He came to bring sight to the blind, to release captives, to set the downtrodden free. He seems to want something of this type of clear focus or vision from us too: 'Because you are neither hot nor cold I spit you out of my mouth' (Mk 10:51). That's tough to hear! If we took this too literally, we might bully ourselves into doing things *we think* God is demanding of us. I am consoled when I am reminded that the spirit comes to help us in our weakness.

I was sitting beside the indoor swimming pool in the hotel. I was trying to make a difficult decision, between what I thought God was asking of me and what I wanted myself. I noticed a couple with a toddler; they were trying to put the toddler into the water. Each time they lowered him towards the water, he resisted, kicking and screaming vehemently, shouting 'No!' They continued to try to lower him in, and he continued to scream. I felt so sorry for the child, being pushed beyond what he felt he was able for. Eventually, after many failed attempts, the father gathered the toddler into his arms and wrapped him in a large, soft, fluffy towel. The child snuggled into relaxation. After a while, the father started to take handfuls of water from the pool and playfully dribbled some onto the child's forehead, whereby the child giggled happily. Eventually, the giggling evolved into a belly laugh, so caught up was the child with the water pouring down his face. After a while I heard a loud splash – no resistance this time, and the toddler was in the water, still belly laughing!

Resistance

Previously, the whole concept of resistance puzzled me and I tried to 'push through it' rather than listen to and integrate it. I am now seeing how resistance is always at play in our journey of growth – right from the beginning, when we resisted being born, and in all those moments when we internally or externally screamed 'No!' Resistance could be defined as 'an unconscious response that is part of all normal growth in which the person avoids some issue, some experience, or some insight by some form of avoiding behaviour'.[48]

All relationships have interplay of connection and disconnection, growth and resistance. Sometimes, we notice how we resist feedback or challenges from friends, especially when they are catalysts for change or raising awareness. This resistance, if ignored, can create a gradual lessening of aliveness or realness in our contact. We can use subtle defences, like talking about things 'out there', as a kind of defence. However, 'sometimes resistance is good protection. There are patterns inherent in spiritual growth that support readiness for certain opportunities or challenges at specific times.'[49]

Light and Shadow

But my face, he said, you cannot see, for no human being can see me and survive. (Ex 33:20)

Sometimes the light is too dazzling and we're not ready for it so we resist. In his inauguration speech, Nelson Mandela said

---

[48] Janet K. Ruffing, *Spiritual Direction: Beyond the Beginnings* (London: St Pauls Publishing, 2000), p. 33.

[49] Jeannette A. Bakke, *Holy Invitations: Exploring Spiritual Direction* (Michigan: Baker Books, 2000), p. 25.

'it is our light not our darkness that frightens us'. Scripture tells us likewise: 'Though the light has come into the world, people have preferred darkness to the light' (Jn 3:19). When we try to protect our self-image – the image we have constructed of ourselves – we often try to stay with the safe and familiar, avoiding exposure. Sometimes we get stuck between the dream and the action. We must never attack the defences or even refer to the resistance in confrontational ways. Like the child, in resisting the water and being calmed by the embrace of her father, we too need the Divine embrace in our resistance so that eventually we can begin to take baby steps. The spirit does not break us in our resistance – that is the activity of our own inner critic. We will discover what we are to do when the desire of the heart wells up from within. We can discern this desire when we sift through the inner and outer experiences in our lives, and it will not feel like we are being thrown into the water alone and terrorised. More likely, our life's calling will come within our places of delight, where, like the toddler in the pool, we find ourselves giggling, and where we know we are wrapped in the enfolding love of God. Ignatius of Loyola, who developed much around the area of discernment, talks about our *unity of desires,* where our own dream and God's dream are as one (because we have moved beyond surface desires of the false self). 'I tell you the truth, my father will grant you anything you ask in my name' (Jn 16:23).

Taking a path towards wholeness inevitably means a challenge that can feel threatening to old ways of being. 'Jesus frequently presses the people closest to him into places they find threatening. He functions repeatedly as a boundary-crosser, pushing his disciples to edges they find exceedingly uncomfortable.'[50]

Resistance can come in the form of avoidance, repression, denial or forgetting. We can also overwork or 'over anything' as a form of resistance. We avoid facing our resistance and its

---

[50] Belden C. Lane, *The Solace of Fierce Landscapes* (New York: Oxford University Press, 1998), p. 46.

associated feelings; we feel more distant from God, others and ourselves. Many people choose to go for spiritual direction or talk to a trusted friend about their own issues of resistance. Paradoxically, we can resist talking about our resistance. I have memories of times where I wanted to cancel a spiritual direction session (or hoped my spiritual director would cancel), and noticed in hindsight that these sessions were often the most significant or fruitful; 'the things we are most reluctant to discuss in spiritual direction are often the things that need care and attention'.[51] When feelings of resistance are listened to, something changes; 'perhaps all the dragons in our life are princesses who are only waiting to see us act, just once, with beauty and courage'.[52]

We can become aware of how resistance, in its many guises, is a movement taking us away from a God encounter. Ignatius points out, in rules for discernment, how we move away from consolation and become attracted to a distraction that is actually a form of desolation. We are all wrestling with our attraction and resistance to what is truly life giving. Our fear of change and our fear of exposure is quiet primal and so we need to befriend this dynamic in ourselves – not to get rid of anything, but to bring ourselves to the loving gaze of God who touches our resistance like the sun melts the snow.

Reflection

Where does resistance show up in your life? What does it feel like? How does it prevent you from growing and from taking risks? What function is it serving, what might be its protective mechanism? If there is a situation in your life now where there is resistance, maybe you can bring it to deeper awareness, give it a shape, an image, and explore what you are afraid of. Bring this awareness to your prayer, don't push beyond your resistance, just bring it to compassionate mindfulness. When you do this, it will change, you will change.

---

[51] Jeannette A. Bakke, *Holy Invitations: Exploring Spiritual Direction*, p. 25.
[52] Daniel J. O'Leary, *Travelling Light: Your Journey to Wholeness* (Dublin: Columba Press, 2001), p. 53.

CHAPTER 22

Joyful Mysteries:
Discovering What Brings Us Joy

*It doesn't interest me how old you are. I want to
know if you will risk looking like a fool for love, for
your dream, for the adventure of being alive.*[53]

ORIAH MOUNTAIN

I knew of a seventy-five-year-old lady starting off a four-year counselling psychotherapy training course around the same time as I was doing a similar course. A fellow student asked her, 'But what age will you be when you graduate?' 'The same age I will be if I don't graduate,' she replied. She died less than a year after graduation. What a shame, some said, just as her dream was starting. What a miracle, others said, just as she fulfilled her dream. It is not what we see, but how we see. It does not matter what age we are or what our status is, once we awaken to the dream within us.

The adventure of being alive calls us to live in uncertainty where the only certainty is change and death – two of the things we resist the most. Sometimes we are accused of being 'depressing' or 'morbid' when we talk about death, and yet an acceptance of our mortality and awareness of the brevity of life brings more passion, joy and enthusiasm to life. Living as if it is your last day on earth can infuse an ordinary day with a sense of gratitude and an urgency to live and taste every

---

[53] Oriah Mountain, 'Dreamer', p. 1.

moment more fully, whether or not we graduate at the end of it.

Expectation and Disappointment

Fixed expectations can leave us feeling that this moment or experience isn't good enough (in other words, it doesn't meet the expectations we had built up around it). So while an experience may be wonderful in itself, if it is held up against the picture of what we expected it to be, or what we thought it should be, it will inevitably disappoint us. Life as it should be is often at odds with life just as it is. Perhaps this explains why Christmas is high on the list of what stresses us – we often have high expectations of what a perfect Christmas looks and feels like. There is an ocean of distress caused by checking everything against the invisible measuring tape of our expectations. Fixed expectations and comparisons rob life of its joy and mystery. By tending to the soil of our inner landscapes and attempting to uproot some of the weeds of our inflexible and rigid expectations, we can help our natural happiness to blossom. Our joy then becomes like a magnet, drawing happy people and happy circumstances towards us. 'If you commit to joy, the law of attraction will pour an avalanche of joyful things, people, circumstances, events and opportunities into your life, all because you are radiating joy.'[54]

Bed of Roses

I looked around the lovely teahouse, with its beautiful arrangement of pottery, the lovely old-world style dresser filled with pretty china. I looked out the window at the bed of roses near the hedge in the amazing garden, overlooking the sea. *Living in a bed of roses*, I mused, as I enviously watched the owner introduce her guests to her lovely array of home baking, smiling graciously as she did so, receiving each of the compliments offered to her regarding this beautiful place. *Lucky*

---

[54] Jack Canfield, quoted in *The Secret* by Rhonda Byrne (New York: Atria Books, 2006), p. 179.

thing, I thought, *I would love to live in this beautiful place.* I visualised what it must be like to wake up here each day. My thoughts were punctuated by a conversation at the table nearby. 'Isn't she marvellous,' one remarked, 'it is so lovely to see the teahouse is open today, she so often has to close it when she spends such long spells of time in hospital.' 'Yes, depression is a terrible thing,' the other replied. After that day I was less inclined to presume that someone else lived *in a bed of roses*; I now avoid creating such idealistic or envious pictures of those who seem to have it all.

Matthieu Ricard, in his book *Happiness,* says that 'one of the main sources of people's discontent comes from comparing themselves with others, in their family, at their work place, and among their acquaintances'.[55] We cannot enjoy the present moment while we are looking over our shoulder wondering if someone else is having it better. While one person may seem to be getting a bigger slice of the cake, we would do well to remind ourselves that there is someone else who has no cake.

Attitudes of Gratitude

'We are all in the gutter, but some of us are looking at the stars,' Oscar Wilde once said. Raining again, I thought to myself disappointedly, it's raining on my holidays, when I was looking forward to some nice sunshine. A little bit of self-pity was creeping in and I was spiralling into the gutter of the 'poor me' scenario, until my thoughts were interrupted by a phone call from a friend, Margaret, who was completing her cancer treatment. She was ringing to let me know that she was taking the three dogs, which she had rescued, to be assessed as therapy dogs, so that, she excitedly explained, she could visit nursing homes and hospitals and bring some joy to others. These last few years, her kitchen was taken over by abandoned puppies, now big dogs, which she was taking to visit people who felt alone. The Chernobyl child who was now living with her was

---

[55] Matthieu Ricard, *Happiness: A Guide to Developing Life's Most Important Skill* (London: Atlantic Books, 2003), p. 173.

helping her to wash them. Rescue puppies, abandoned child, recovering from cancer – Margaret had no time for self pity; she is one of those who is *looking towards the stars*. When I asked her about the secret of her happiness, Margaret replied, 'Having cancer was actually a gift in my life. I now live fully in the moment. I have so much contentment and happiness, and I don't hold onto money or hold onto anything anymore. Simple things bring joy: looking out at the fields, watching the dogs play, just being grateful for everything brings such happiness.'

Research on Happiness

We often feel if we could have a more affluent lifestyle, live in a nicer location, have more sunny weather, we would be happy. However, according to current research on happiness psychology, it is not a change in circumstances or the accumulation of things or achievements or even another person that can raise our level of happiness. The pleasurable feelings associated with these changes or acquired possessions fade rapidly once the external stimulus disappears. 'Happiness is not just about obtaining momentary subjective states. Happiness also includes the idea that one's life has been authentic.'[56] People often talk about the weather being depressing in Ireland, yet surprisingly, research reveals that those who have moved to a warmer climate are not all necessarily happier. Everyone is interested in learning how to increase levels of happiness. A few years ago my husband did a research thesis on the study of happiness. I couldn't wait to hear the results of his research, and was somewhat disappointed when I heard repeatedly that discipline, commitment to a goal, having a sense of purpose or contribution, as well as the delaying of gratification, featured highly on the list of ingredients of what brings happiness. I expected his research would show that

---

[56] Martin Seligman, *Authentic Happiness: Using the New Positive Psychology to Realise Your Potential for Lasting Fulfilment* (New York: Free Press Publications, 2002), p. 262.

happiness came from such things as positive affirmations, happy thoughts and a healthy lifestyle. While self-acceptance, nurturing relationships, spirituality and present moment living featured highly, I was surprised to learn how significant the ability to delay or postpone instant pleasure for the pursuit of something more noble or a greater cause was on the list. While words like 'discipline' and 'delayed gratification' do not sound like much fun, and are not for the faint-hearted, these concepts are grounded in solid research.

Having spent over ten years studying psychology and psychotherapy, I felt I had spent long enough studying pain, trauma and anxiety, as well as exploring what was wrong or missing in our lives, and had not put enough emphasis on looking at what was good or working well and therefore contributing to well-being. I felt I needed to study what causes happiness rather than what causes depression, and decided to embark on an exploration of positive psychology, life coaching and the principles of neuro-linguistic programming. I came across some very exciting concepts. No matter how difficult our past has been or whatever our learned helplessness, we have an innate ability to visualise something better for ourselves, to choose our attitudes, and create a life based on what inspires us, and what gives us a sense of purpose and congruence with our chosen values. The research done in the fields of positive psychology remind us that counting our blessings, believing in something greater than ourselves and having a goal or something to work towards all contribute to a meaningful life. Also, facing adversity, practicing altruism, overcoming inner demons, working on meaningful relationships, and holding an attitude of optimism all significantly contribute to happiness. Martin Seligman, who has developed and promoted the field of positive psychology since 2000, has been building on the works of Rogers, Maslow and Erikson. Rogers believed humans are positive creatures who inherently move towards fully functioning wholeness. Maslow believed that we have instinctual needs arranged in a hierarchy of importance, and so we achieve actualisation through working through these needs.

Seligman builds on the theories of his predecessors and suggests that most people 'want to live their lives imbued with meaning and not just to fidget until they die'.[57]

If Only

Most of us have a list of if onlys. If only I could lose weight, change job, move to a better house. We assume that we will be happier when these needs are met. Yet research tells us that people who win the lottery are, in the long run, no happier than they were before the win. Perhaps, if we ask ourselves to remember when we ourselves were at our happiest in life, we will gain our own wisdom. While it is generally understood that much of our personality traits are attributable to genetic inheritance, there is a lot we can change by altering our attitudes and by committing to new and more life-giving habits and patterns.

One of Those Days

'Don't bother going to school today, sure it's raining outside.' These words were spoken to me by my mother, on more than one occasion, on school mornings. I must have been the envy of every child. I would snuggle back under the bed clothes (I had been half expecting there would be no school anyway once I had heard the rain). 'I don't have time to wash your face this morning, so you can stay in bed,' was another one I remember. Not having to have my face scrubbed, but most of all not having to go to school and explain why I hadn't done my homework, was a great relief.

Unfortunately, during my life, I have continued to use varied applications of 'sure it's raining', for example, when the thought comes to take some exercise, or do some gardening. Likewise, when I reach for yet another chocolate, the excuse can be transferred to 'sure it's Christmas', or 'sure it's the weekend'. The excuse, of course, is usually accompanied by a resolve to change all those habits next week, next month, but

---

[57] Ibid.

not now, *sure it's raining*. I have sometimes vowed to make lifetime changes tomorrow or next week, promising myself I will finally do all the things I have been putting off. Have you ever, like me, thrown yet another newspaper on to the old pile of papers on the couch and say 'one of these days I'll clear all these away', or have you ever sneaked a second slice of cream cake, promising yourself that 'one of these days I will cut out all the sugar'? We so often imagine that *one of these days* we will magically clear the backlog of our bad habits and do all the things we have dreamed we'll get around to doing. Unfortunately, there is rarely any magical *one of these days*; rather, it is the daily application of ourselves to the little tasks and goals that create change.

I learnt this more powerfully recently when I was attending a physiotherapist for my injured ankle. Each week she would patiently ask if I had done the prescribed exercises, which I usually hadn't because I was convincing myself that time would heal it and that I would be out walking in no time. It is great to have a compelling vision for *one fine day*, but the visualisation needs to be accompanied by the setting and accomplishment of daily tasks, persistently directed towards that actualisation of that vision. Likewise, we need to have small, measurable targets, just enough to challenge us, and inspire us, but not to overstretch us, or we will not be able to stay with the momentum. I learned this the hard way when I decided, 'Ok, I'll really apply myself to the goal of making my ankle strong', so I bought an exercise bike and with great zeal I turned the wheel up to high speed and started peddling like mad, until, snap, my knee jammed. The unused muscles were stretched too much and I injured my knee. So there I was, no longer just nursing a painful ankle but now also a painful knee – and painful pride, as I discarded the 'useless bike', not to be used again.

We often start off with great enthusiasm, and peddle like mad towards the fulfilment of our dreams, until our energy wanes and we feel that familiar gravitational pull towards the comfort zone. This is when we often buckle at the first fence of adversity, but our resilience and resolve to overcome the demons within will get us through this stage. The demons can say, 'What is the point? It's too late now, nobody can really change.' Likewise, we can hold disempowering beliefs (like those that suggest that life should be fair, and that we should get special privileges because of our difficult past). Consequently, we often secretly feel that we shouldn't have to work so hard at our happiness. We can then slump back into learnt helplessness, victimise ourselves in feelings of hopelessness and self-doubt, and, in so doing, the easier option is subordinated to our deeper desire to grow. While wanting to choose the easy route is understandable, it leaves us without inner motivation, weakens our self-efficacy, and robs us of self-mastery.

Reflection
Reflect on a time when you felt at peace, happy as if you were in the flow of life. What were you doing? What beliefs or attitudes did you employ at that time? Were you adhering to the fulfilment of a particular goal or dream? What were you grateful for? Reflect on what brought you happiness on that occasion. Perhaps you can bring some of that to a present circumstance that is difficult.

CHAPTER 23

Working with Attitude:
The Ripple Effect

What lies behind us and what lies before us are tiny matters compared to what lies within us.

OLIVER WENDELL HOLMES

Two minutes late. The airline check-in desk had closed. We had pre-booked a ticket from Cork to Dublin and now we were not allowed to board. Angrily, I went to the information desk, to be told that all we could do was book another flight with another airline that was departing shortly. That would cost another sixty euro. 'Ridiculous,' I fumed, 'what bad luck!' A man next to us was in the same situation. However, his reaction was somewhat different: 'Oh great, there is another flight soon! What good luck, I'll still get to my destination in time.' I looked at him and thought him to be in denial, not being able to see that he was being ripped off.

I begrudgingly paid the sixty euro and caught the next flight. I was going to a coaching seminar on 'workplace and organisational spirituality', and guess who was there, in the same discussion group as me? As part of our work one day, he was asked to share the secret of his thriving business in recessionary times. 'It's all about attitude,' he said. 'I always choose to feel grateful, to seek the possibility in every setback, and to count my blessings.' I hoped he wouldn't recognise me!

Opening the Gates of Change

Marilyn Ferguson, in *The Aquarian Conspiracy: Personal and Social Transformation in the 1980s*, writes: 'No one can persuade another to change, each of us guards a gate of change that can only be opened from the inside.'[58] We can open the gates of change when we freely choose ways of being, and attitudes that are congruent with our deepest values. Personal transformation can bring a revolution, not just within, but around us – in organisations, workplaces and communities. When we live with more gratitude, inner directedness, integrity and self-definition, we infuse the world around us with positivity and proactivity – creating a workplace culture that is more guided by principles than one motivated by the 'fear of being found out'. Self-awareness and reflection lead us to the discovery of a core deep within us, that is, in some respect, changeless – no longer defined by what everyone else thinks of us or by passing fashion or trends, but built on chosen values and attitudes.

The Beatitudes invite us to enter into and internalise a blueprint that acts as a buffer to society's demands, as well as the demands created by the dictates of our own egos, which compel us to push, compete, succeed, manipulate. Through reflection, we learn how our response to the world around us does not have to be reactive or controlled by following popular trends, but can be value-based, and we can learn to subordinate moods, feelings, impulses to these selected values. With awareness, we can be the observer of our own responses, thus exercising internal power. This inner blueprint and inner authority is also crucial to good leadership, as without it we cannot empower others. When leaders are insecure and looking for outside validation and popularity, there is a lack of integrity and truth in the organisation. Likewise, when leaders are operating from a hierarchical system and grasping status or control, there is an atmosphere of domination and

---

[58] Marilyn Ferguson, *The Aquarian Conspiracy: Personal and Social Transformation in the 1980s* (New York: Penguin, 2009), p. 112.

defensiveness engendered around them. Employees become outwardly submissive but inwardly rebellious, which creates a negative and dangerous energy in the workplace.

When an organisation or community is guided by a clear sense of mission and positive attitude at the forefront, there is an expansive, positive and creative atmosphere engendered. Only then can there be possibility of everyone living out of something purposeful and life giving. As well as it being important to adopt positive attitudes and inner integrity, we must discover our imagination – that which enables us to visualise a reality beyond our present one. We need to see glimpses of the uncreated worlds of limitless potential which are possible. Through creative visualisation, we can channel our most difficult circumstances and forge from them our greatest triumphs. There is something inherently attractive about people who have reflected on difficult life events, overcome obstacles, chosen values to live by, and who today embody and engender a unique presence because of their attitude. As Oliver Wendell Holmes said, 'What lies behind us and what lies before us are tiny matters compared to what lies within us.'

Reflection
Find a quiet place to be by yourself. Reflect on an area where you feel stuck in your life, maybe where you feel in a rut. Maybe you are blaming someone else or circumstances for this dilemma you find yourself in. If so, just acknowledge whatever you feel, whilst also being aware of any disempowering beliefs you hold.

Gradually allow a picture to emerge of how this situation could be different. See it in your mind's eye as if you are now calling it into being. Now decide on one small action you can take today to transport yourself toward this dream.

CHAPTER 24

Happy Ever After: Searching for the Treasure

We shall not cease from exploration
And the end of all our exploring
Will be to arrive where we started
And know the place for the first time.[59]

T. S. ELIOT

I love fairytales. Indeed I enjoy them more as an adult than I did as a child. There is something about the 'once upon a time' that makes us all sit up and listen, and about the 'happily ever after' that soothes our fears. Fairytales can teach us many things: that goodness can triumph over evil, light over darkness, kindness over greed. The heroes or heroines do not become so because they have been powerful, proud or influential, but because they remain loyal to certain values or virtues and don't give in to a less virtuous shortcut. Values remain at the centre of the fairytale and commitment to these values often involves slaying a dragon, vanquishing a witch, crossing a deep river, or suffering a time of confinement. The 'treasure' found at the end is no handout, no piece of good luck or inheritance, but is gained as a consequence of overcoming obstacles in the pursuit of some noble goal. We tend to wish for a 'happy ever after' without any pain, security without losses, a life without death, but the fairytale shows us that it is in embracing our vulnerability and mortality and facing obstacles

---

[59] T. S. Eliot, *Four Quartets, The Complete Poems and Plays of T. S. Eliot* (London: Faber & Faber, 2004).

that we live life with more joy and consequently with less anxiety. Kindness, goodness, beauty, love and honesty are emulated as the treasures found at the end of the journey in fairytales, and the 'quick fixes' often promised by greed, pride, power or cruelty do not win out. The 'happy ever after' is more about integration, peace following conquest, harmony found and discovered through doing the journey, against all the odds.

The hero inside all of us is ignited when listening to a fairytale. We discover that when we dig deep within, we find the treasure – that spark inside us that can transcend obstacles, face adversity, confront demons and win through, no matter what our circumstances or past might have been. We no longer hand over our fate to another or wait to get lucky someday, but with renewed resilience we confront the demons and wicked witches of our own limiting self-belief; we do battle with what tries to hold us back; we face the obstacles, believing they can in fact make us stronger. When we are offered easy solutions, we must stay true to our deeper values and define our own happy ever after, which is not dependent on perfect circumstances or on things going our way. Rather, we discover an inner peace by taking the courageous path that leads to transformation.

Seeing Anew

We discover that it is often in the dark times, we discover that 'God was in this place and I knew it not' (Gn 28:16). We discover that each encounter, each experience was part of the whole. When we see the big picture, the fairytale of our own lives, we learn that even the mistakes were transformed into something beautiful. We discover that the seeming tragedies could not quench the indestructible life force within us. In fact, we discover that the only real tragedy would have been to lose our inner perseverance – that which got us through the heartaches, even on those times when we thought we could not rise again. We marvel at how the winters may have knocked us, yet something in us rose up and blossomed for yet one more spring.

The roses outside my window never looked as beautiful as they do this year. They stand up with such dignity, displaying unapologetically their beautiful colour and giving off their wonderful fragrance. I have wondered why they look especially beautiful this year (although I also notice that some of those from last year have died). I am no gardener, but am wondering if it could be because of the exceptional hard winter, when frost attacked them, and so those that survived had to dig down deeper into the soil for strength. Most of us know what that feels like: when we look back, we marvel at how our unquenchable spirit survived, how the hero inside of us climbed our own Mount Everest, even on those occasions when the world seemed to walk away and leave us bleeding – we didn't just survive, like the roses, we dug deep within and found a new strength, and quietly celebrated our newly discovered dignity, resilience and wisdom. We might even thank our adversaries and bless our enemies for the gift they have given in aiding us to find those wonderful treasures buried deep within the soil of our own being.

When we look back, we discover that some amazing energy must have ran through our veins, 'the same stream of life that runs through my veins night and day runs through the world and dances in rhythmic measures'.[60] When we look back with the eyes of the soul, we see that oftentimes it was when we were weak we were strong, and when we were last we were first. We discover that we were blessed when we mourned, and happy when we were persecuted, and wise when we were foolish. These 'upside-down contradictions' seem like foolishness to the ego, but to the spirit they are pure wisdom.

May you have holy wisdom guiding you as she invites you to listen, so that you may find the treasure, one deeper than any earthly riches.

And so I prayed and wisdom was given to me; I entreated, and the spirit of wisdom came to me. I esteemed her more than sceptres and thrones; compared with her I held riches as nothing. I reckoned no precious stone to be her equal, for compared with her; all gold is a pinch of sand and beside

---

[60] Rabindranath Tagore, 'Stream of Life', *Gitanjali* (Minneapolis: Filiquarian Publishing LLC, 2007), p. 49.

her, silver ranks as mud. I loved her more than health or beauty, preferred her to the light, since her radiance never sleeps. (Wis 7:7-11)

As we continue to create the fairytale of our lives, may we never forget to leave some crumbs behind us on the path that we have travelled. Like the crumbs left behind by Hansel and Gretel, some, who may follow after us, may find direction when they see the crumbs of wisdom on the trail we have left behind. 'What I learned diligently, I shall pass on liberally, I shall not conceal how rich she is' (Wis 7:13).

We are all subject, now and then, to being lured by a 'candy house' and mistaking it for the real thing. There is always a danger we might get weary and so give up the search too soon and settle for that candy, and God forbid that we would settle – settle for anything less than the horizons for which we were created. Remember, there may be somebody, somewhere, facing a dragon or a witch, or they may be lost in a forest and don't know where the path is. It may just be because of those crumbs of wisdom you left behind, they might keep trusting, keep persevering on the path for another while. When they are lost in a forest, they might be consoled to know that there is an opening somewhere, and others have trod this way before.

So, do not throw away your treasure – and, more importantly, do not throw away yourself. Don't worry about what ages or dulls the skin, be concerned only with what ages and dulls your spirit. And remember: it is never too late to start living the unlived fairytale of your life – you might start to feel young at eighty, even if you felt old at forty.

Reflection

If you were to visualise your own life as a fairytale, what title would you give to it? What will you, as the hero of your story, have overcome or achieved in pursuit of the treasure? What unique trail will you have left behind – like crumbs of nourishment on the path that you have trod? Maybe you can begin today to reflect on and to write your fairytale, and don't forget to enjoy your very own 'happy ever after'.